Talking with Angels of Light

Talking with Angels of Light

Embrace your Truth

AMANDA HART

S

First published in Great Britain in 2019 by Orion Spring
an imprint of The Orion Publishing Group Ltd
Carmelite House, 50 Victoria Embankment
London EC4Y 0DZ

An Hachette UK Company

1 3 5 7 9 10 8 6 4 2

A CIP catalogue record for this book
is available from the British Library.

ISBN (Mass market paperback) 978 1 4091 8102 6
ISBN (eBook) 978 1 4091 8103 3

Printed and bound in Great Britain by Clays Ltd, Elcograf S.p.A.

www.orionbooks.co.uk

Contents

Introduction

'Where are you?' I ask myself
I hear but can't quite see.
A thought, a touch, a dream, a glow
I feel you there with me.

What are angels?

If you look at the definition of 'angel' in the Oxford English Dictionary, it says, '*A spiritual being believed to act as an attendant, agent, or messenger of God, conventionally represented in human form with wings and a long robe.*'

Angels come to us in different ways. Some of you may have already experienced a variety of meaningful angel communications. Some may have even experienced them through near-death experiences. Angels have an incredible way of communicating their love for us when we are truly open to their existence.

Angels are 'beings of light', as some believe they use light's electromagnetic energy to travel to our physical world from the energy world, spirit or Divine. Angels of light are messengers from what I refer to as Source.

Source is the creator of all things, the fountain of all knowledge, the powerful life force that supports, nurtures and recreates humanity, the animal kingdom and everything that resides in living form on earth. Many people theorise that it's all down to science, but many also believe that creation is constructed and influenced by Source or whatever our belief is — God, the Divine, the Supreme Being, Elohim, Allah, Brahman, Buddha, or many other terms depending on your faith or religion. It matters not. Whatever you believe in, I refer to this creator force as Source (which is not defined by religion or culture) throughout the book, because I believe that we are all connected, regardless of our beliefs, cultures or upbringings.

Types of angels

There are types of angels such as archangels, cherubim, seraphim, dominions, principalities, and so on. Then there are specific angels to help us with certain aspects of our life, for example Archangel Michael for protection, Archangel Gabriel for communication and Archangel Chamuel for love and relationships. Angels have been acknowledged in certain religions such as Christianity where angels are mentioned throughout the Old and New Testaments and referred to as spiritual beings who serve God. According to the sacred writings of the Koran in the Muslim religion, an angel in the form of a man guided Muhammad in the development of his faith. In Buddhism, angels are referred to as 'devas' and in Hinduism as 'the shining ones'.

Angelology

Angelology, the study of angels, has been around for centuries. It's not that we only discovered it at a certain time, but that we as a human race were compelled to study what we'd always known, recognising that angels have always been with us.

When we look back to ancient civilisations, painted, winged entities were discovered on Egyptian tombs. There are also many stories of angels and studies conducted throughout medieval history, because they had become so important during the Middle Ages.

Throughout history, different angels have been talked about including through theology, the study of the nature of the Divine. Many spiritual teachers and famous leaders have spoken about receiving angelic guidance, including Jesus, Muhammad, Socrates, George Washington, Da Vinci, Ralph Waldo Emerson, Joan of Arc, Saint Bernadette of Lourdes and Carl Jung among many others. Emanuel Swedenborg, John Milton, Thomas Aquinas and False Dionysius are among the leading angel writers and philosophers in history. The classical writings of Dante, Milton, Goethe and Shakespeare have also inspired contemporary writers who continue to share their stories about angels.

Today there is a resurgence in angelology during a period in history when, I believe, humanity needs their guidance more than ever.

About me

I had my first encounter with angels when I was about three years old. I was sent to my father's house and told I had to live there, away from Mum, quite suddenly and unexpectedly. I arrived in a world so alien to the one I'd known before, which introduced fear, uncertainty and confusion into my existence.

I prayed for help on that first night as I lay in my unfamiliar bed in strange, new surroundings — not because I knew who or what I was praying to, but because it was something I'd seen my grandmother do, and she always seemed to receive the help she needed.

'Dear Angels,' I prayed, *'I know you always help my grandma as she talks about you all the time, so please can you help me too? I'm frightened and miss my mummy and all my family.'*

My first angel visited me in a dream that night and soon became an important recurring dream throughout my childhood. In the dream, I was always taken on a journey to a place that I had no prior knowledge of: a place with vast areas of parkland in a town with a common that had paths criss-crossing through it. I would fly over this common, hovering above it before diving, twisting and soaring up into the sky and back down again, exploring my great ability to be *free*.

In the dream I was never alone; it was my 'safe place' to meet and play with my new-found angel friends whom I quickly grew to love and named 'The Guys Upstairs', as I thought they lived in our attic. I knew they were my angels, sent to love, guide and protect me.

As the rest of my childhood unfolded, it became apparent why my angels came to me. My days spent living with my father's family were like a dark prison and were volatile. I prayed that my angel friends would help me through the pains I experienced in my waking state and, little by little, I started to see, hear and feel their presence around me, as they guided me into the light.

'Amanda, we're always here to guide and protect you. You only need to call on us whenever you need our help.' They assured me.

My father raised me as a Christian, however, as I developed my spirituality as an adult, I realised that my faith was no longer restricted to a single religion and was supported by a belief that we are all influenced by a universal energy that unifies and bonds us as one entire race.

I learned how to communicate more frequently with my angels and managed to survive my tough childhood thanks to their unwavering love and support. Miraculously I overcame many explosive situations, which I couldn't possibly have endured without their help. My journey into adulthood was also rough and, at times, a terrifying 'daymare', and my resilience and determination to keep my head up was only possible because of my relationship with my angels, who guided me through many dark tunnels of difficulty with their loving light.

I knew in the depths of my soul that whatever I had to face in life my angels would face it with me, and this realisation of their unconditional love is where my real spiritual journey began.

I spent many years changing the negative habits (scars) I had developed during my turbulent upbringing. I did whatever I could to enhance my angelic relationships and support my spiritual, mental, emotional and physical wellbeing. I studied reiki and other healing methods — massage techniques, crystals, reflexology, hypnotherapy, past life regression, meditation and flower essences. I learned about certain religions, affirmations, mantras and prayer. I built altars and collected talismans. I went to workshops by the bucketload, absorbed countless self-help and spiritual development books until I'd amassed a library, and attended the Spiritual Church, development groups and one-to-one training. I visited numerous sacred sites such as Avebury, Glastonbury and the temples and pyramids in Egypt. I went on to help clients and taught classes. I found my true path, my calling and my tribe, and my life changed from a dark, frightening and lonely existence to one of light, joy and purpose, supported by beautiful people who I love and adore and who love me in return.

Even through the tough times, my angels constantly reassured me with *'You are never alone Amanda. We're always with you.'*

I have helped countless clients over the past twenty years to communicate with their angels. I have written this book under the guidance of my own angels of light with the aim of enabling you to activate or deepen your communication with your own angels of light. My mission here is to help you see you are never alone and will always be able to draw upon their guidance to help you navigate the uncertainties of life — whether they be in the home, at work or elsewhere.

We live in an unpredictable world where challenges are inevitable. We all go through times when we feel abandoned, cut off and afraid. However, we can decide how we deal with life's shortcomings: we can either struggle along and make our own fear-based decisions or we can stand aside and allow our angels of light to assist us and teach us the lessons we need to heal, grow and create the right outcomes for our highest good.

Our angels provide a rich source of help and solutions and will help you to lead an authentic life according to your blueprint. The **blueprint** of our soul is like an instruction manual on how to become our best self with a trouble-shooting section built in to help us learn vital lessons to help navigate us towards the essence of who we are and our truth.

I was amazed when I discovered I had a blueprint: we all do from birth, containing all information that would be crucial for us to survive. The animal and plant kingdoms work with the same principle and are perfectly in harmony as they honour their blueprint and know how to reproduce themselves in alignment with the polyphony of the planet.

Consciousness, another term for the energy world, contains all information about who you've been, who you are now and who you will be in the future based on your potential choices. Consciousness matches the detail it has on record with our blueprint like a fingerprint match, so when we allow our angels to guide us, they already know our best self, better than we know ourselves. So now it's time for you to get to know your angels!

Who this book is for

This book is for the inquisitive who are searching for more meaning in their lives and want to communicate with their angels. It is for anyone who wants a richer and more fulfilling relationship with their angels. It's even for those who've never felt close to the angel realm but who want to open that door.

Our angels of light are there to make us giggle, to spread joy and to move us away from the heaviness of our lives. With joy we're far better equipped to create a life of beauty — I should know this as I spent much of my life afraid, isolated and battling various mental health problems. I hope your angels of light will open your heart and mind to the wonders of the human condition and the amazing world we live in. This book will help you to connect with your angels who will allow you to see how adaptable, powerful and incredibly resourceful we humans truly are.

My angels are my best friends, my dearest allies, my fountain of knowledge and my shoulder to cry on. Building your own relationship with your angels of light is like having a hundred personal assistants working for you to better your life, each specialising in various aspects of your world with expert advice.

I want you to develop the same relationship with your own angels and to believe that they are, and always will be, by your side, helping you to help others make this world a better place for us *all* to live in.

Why angels expand our life experience

When we connect through our angels to Source, we recognise that we are, in fact, all the same. We all try to get through life the best way we can, searching for the right path in order to navigate our personal journeys. When we deepen our connection to our angels, our path becomes lighter, it flows with the rhythm of life and tunes us into our destiny. Regardless of our upbringings, when we tune into our messengers, we have the ability to hear the wisdom of Source to help steer us onwards through the rocky terrain and the storms of life. We can connect with our angels despite religious belief, race or nationality as angels have been around long before any religion was ever formed.

How to use this book

This book is designed to be read again and again so you can draw on it throughout your life, whenever you need it most. We live in a fast-paced world as it is, so this book is supposed to help you take the foot off the accelerator enough for you to listen and pay attention to your angel communication. For me, spirituality is not about spending hours taking part in rituals that just add to your busyness and stress so I have incorporated the following practical elements into this book, which will enhance your angelic communication.

Your light bulb moment

Do you remember the simple electricity circuits we used to make in science classes at school, where the light bulb would not shine if there were any tiny holes or 'faults' in the circuit? Consider this simple experiment as an analogy of your own spiritual awakening. If you are carrying any fears, underlying assumptions, external obstacles or nega-tive memories, they will create 'faults' in your own personal energy circuit and this will stop you from receiving light blessings from your angels. Throughout this book you will find activities that are designed to free your personal energy circuit of any 'faults' so that your angels can actively shine their light on your journey. These activities are **Your light bulb moments** because I hope that they inspire you and enhance the line of communication between you and your angels.

Meditations

Meditation stems from Eastern origins and helps to still the mind and reach a heightened level of awareness. There are so many studies that show that meditation has a huge beneficial effect on the mind and body.

Meditation is an incredibly healing practice, to align us to bring about the 'wholeness'. Mental nutrition is necessary to improve who you wish to be. Healing the internal mind chatter and the outer irritating noise clutter in our life is far more important than you may realise. Meditation has an exceptional way of 'turning down and tuning out' the noise pollution. Many people who live in constant noise or fill their lives with sound to blot out stress, find that once they incorporate meditation, their wellbeing shifts radically and often their lifestyles and relationships change to match their new lighter vibration.

Some of the benefits include reducing stress, anti-ageing, creating appreciation for life, creating more time and improving brain function. It helps you feel connected, helps you sleep well and improves your metabolism. It also increases immunity and fights diseases, increases your attention span and helps with pain relief. Think of meditation as opening a metaphysical door from the physical world into the energy world every time you want to communicate with your angels.

Affirmations

Throughout the book affirmations are included for you to use and incorporate into your daily life in order to create a mindset that is more in alignment with the high vibration of your angels of light. Simply put, affirmations are positive statements in the present tense that you read to yourself in order to create your desires in the future, as if they are your reality now. Angels of light respond to your positive statements and therefore deliver your requests in the form that serves your highest good. You can select and use these affirmations as part of your daily ritual. The best time to read them is first thing in the morning as you wake or last thing at night before you sleep. Angels of light love us to create ritual, so choose what works best for you to suit your lifestyle.

Count your blessings

These notes pages at the end of each chapter provide an opportunity for you to reflect on the many positive things your angels of light are doing for you. They do a lot of things to help you, so it's always worth making time to express your gratitude and thank them for the big and little things as much as possible. Counting your blessings and being grateful for what you have in life shows the Universe that you appreciate and are worthy to receive.

A few things you might want to collect before reading this book

Pen and paper

In my experience, often some of my best angelic communication occurs at the times when I'm most compromised! I can be in the shower in the morning when a solution that I've been struggling with will suddenly come to me from them, which really makes me chuckle. I used to wait until I had finished my shower (or whatever else I was in the middle of doing), in the hope that I would remember their messages later. However, nine times out of ten, my mind would soon fill with other things I needed to do in my day and then I'd forget what they'd tried to tell me. Nowadays, I make sure that I am never far from a pen and paper so I can record my angels' golden nuggets of insight and I suggest you do the same so you can get the most out of this book and from their help.

Talismans

Lucky objects such as a horseshoe, rabbit's foot or charm that are thought to have magic powers have been used for thousands of years to enhance angelic communication. It doesn't matter if your talisman is a pair of lucky old socks, a beloved cuddly toy or a photograph of someone special — it's only important that it is considered lucky to you.

Candles
Candles are commonly used for ceremonies, meditation, prayer and angel connection. Often candles are lit during prayer to bring about positive changes or hope in trying situations.

Crystals
Crystals are used to converse with angels of light as they radiate electromagnetic energy in the same way that light does.

Enjoy the journey!

This book will guide you through the steps to talk with your angels of light, and will enable you to smoothly integrate spiritual changes into the modern world today. Absorb this book, embrace the tools I give you and take my advice into your heart. I only ask that you be open to the whole process and trust me if I push you into uncharted emotional territories. We can't expect change for the better if we only want to do the nice things and avoid the difficult! Being open to your angels of light will take courage, a curious mind, a warm heart and a promise to stop judging yourself along the way.

1

Find the Light

My path is marked with candlelight
To guide me on my way.
No matter how the storms may fare
I know I'll be OK.

Getting started

By reading this book you are already waking to your light or have been aware of it for some time. These are some of the light-based rituals and principles you can easily incorporate into your everyday life before you take the plunge to start trying to communicate with your angels of light.

Light for the physical

- Yoga, t'ai chi, qi gong
- Breath work — Ujjayi or deep breathing
- Walking in nature
- Being close to water
- Cleansing showers

- Salt baths
- Massage and therapeutic touch
- Reflexology, acupuncture, etc.
- Sauna and steam treatments
- A little retail therapy (a new outfit)
- Decluttering
- Nutrition and exercise
- Be mindful of your environment (work and home)
- Positive habits
- Hugging or holding hands with someone you love or respect

Light for the mind

- Meditation
- Relaxation
- Reading
- Creativity
- Visualisation
- Affirmations
- Prayer
- Forgiveness and gratitude
- Mindfulness – thoughts of self and others
- Mindful of what television/Internet content we watch
- Mindful of what we read/ingest
- Positive programmes and beliefs
- Comforting external noises (such as birdsong)
- Soothing or uplifting music

- Learning
- Mandalas
- Colour therapy
- Goals
- Mantras

Light for the emotions

- Right relationships and how they feed us
- Our relationship with our self
- Self-love
- Awareness of what affects our feelings
- Ability to sense what our emotions are teaching us at any given moment, so we can embrace them or make a change
- Spreading kindness to others
- Tithing or giving time/energy to others

Light for the spirit

- The Chakras
- Tools to keep our light bright (crystals, candles, etc.)
- Healing and protection to keep us a pure channel
- Soul work — our own personal journey of discovery
- Workshops, study, books and growth — all chosen through discernment
- Faith
- Journal-keeping
- Energy field

- Compassion towards others and ourselves, the animal and plant kingdoms and the earth
- Sacred space

The symbolism of light

Understanding humanity's relationship with and use of light in our world is important if we want to establish a relationship with our angels of light.

Light and faith

Some of the major religions of the world use light to celebrate the power of God. In Christianity, light is the founding element. The Bible begins with the story of creation in Genesis where light is introduced on the first day: *'God said, "Let there be light," and there was light.'* To this day, Christians continue to use lights to celebrate important festivals, for instance at Christmas twinkling lights everywhere symbolise the birth of Jesus Christ The Saviour. Hindus also light fireworks and burn candles during Diwali to celebrate the triumph of light over darkness. The Jewish holiday of Hanukkah is celebrated by lighting candles on a menorah to mark the revival of the Temple of Jerusalem.

Light and science

When we look back before the scientific revolution (prior to 1543), most technical innovations came from the root of religious traditions. Science affirms that light overpowers darkness in our physical world, because photons in light can dissipate darkness, but darkness cannot dispel light. If you walk into a dark room and turn on a torch, the light will be visible in the darkness even if only a little shines through. In a biological sense, light has fuelled life on our planet from the beginning of time and our ecosystem today still depends on light from the sun. If you consider the food chain: plants contain a pigment called chlorophyll, which gives leaves their green colour and helps the plant to make its food from carbon dioxide, water, nutrients and sunlight energy. This process is called photosynthesis. Animals and humans, further up the food chain, receive their energy from plants, thus making light the essence of all species.

Light and language
Light is often associated with wisdom: to be 'en**light**ened' is to receive knowledge or an understanding. Light also stands for truth and 'spiritually enlightened' people will choose truth over deception, evil or lies. You will notice that the language of light is far spread. Words such as illuminate, brighten, rejuvenation and delightful are positive, uplifting words that embody light. Likewise, we use expressions such as 'feeling **light**-headed' when we come into contact with someone who makes our heart skip a beat of pure joy! Similarly, a person who is '**light**-hearted' is optimistic, cheerful and buoyant. When someone does something '**light**ly' then it means they are behaving in a carefree way.

Angels communicate through us in thought and words every day, although most of us don't ever know it! However, you are reading this book because you have decided to start noticing. A great place to start your relationship with your angels of light is to recognise the language of light in everyday situations. Pay attention to what you are saying to yourself or others, or what people are saying to you and how they are saying it.

The Law of Attraction

For much of my adult life I've been fascinated by the subject of the Law of Attraction and believe that it is one of the greatest universal truths that our angels of light can teach us. It explains that if we focus on positive thoughts we will invite positive experiences into our lives and, adversely, negative thoughts will bring negative experiences, because our thoughts are energy and, as Richard Bach, author of the book, *Illusions*, says 'like attracts like'. Just like the Law of Gravity, the force that attracts us towards the centre of the earth, the Law of Attraction states that our thoughts act as a force, which can attract good or bad experiences depending on what we focus on most.

One of the great 'new thought' leaders of our time, William Walker Atkinson, discovered this when he became unwell, stressed and overwhelmed, working as an attorney in the late 1800s. He had a complete mental, physical and financial breakdown; however, he sought healing which turned his life around. Still continuing with his legal work after his wellness returned, he was inspired to write about how he used mental attraction and other disciplines to make himself well and became a prolific writer in this field, inspiring others to understand about the nature of how we use our mind and the use of our inner senses.

So, if you suffer from an underlying assumption that you are not worthy of the people, situations or things that you truly wish for in your life, or deem the world to be a fearful place, and repeat these mantras over and over in your head, then by this law, you entice your negative subconscious beliefs into your real lived experience. Psychologists and scientists estimate that humans have $60-80,000$ thoughts a day, so if you keep telling yourself *today is a bad day* just imagine how much that can negatively impact your reality. When you have a good day and everything flows it is because you are focusing on the goodness of the day itself. Essentially, what you think about yourself and your situations at this present moment create your future, whether that be from a positive or negative perspective.

Some chapters of my spiritual journey have felt like being repeatedly immersed under water — painful, difficult to breathe, out of control and utterly helpless. As soon as I stopped struggling against the currents and trusted in my angels of light when they reassured me with '*Amanda, you don't need to fight any longer to survive. We will be your guiding light if you trust and let go,*' the process thereafter became a gentle submerging and cleansing, which I welcomed wholeheartedly.

21

The Law of Attraction has certainly taken me on a series of twists and turns in my life but has ultimately enabled me to train with some of the most incredible people who gave me the ability to complete my personal jigsaws and inspired me to help others to complete theirs. Thanks to my angels of light, I am governed by a purpose that is meaningful, truthful and good — like the happy dreams I had as a child.

Becoming aware of your thoughts and words allows you to use them to your advantage. We need to break repeated habits of self-sabotage to attract positive experiences. Talking to my angels of light and asking them for the things I wanted and focusing on those things, eventually attracted them to me, even when my fear-based self thought it was impossible. I allowed my thoughts of what I asked for from my angels to be my dominant thinking.

So, what we say to our angels is as important as the thoughts we process in our minds or think aloud. I like to think that becoming mindful about how we speak to our angels and to ourselves is the most important step in this process. Think of it like gently pulling the reins of a galloping horse and slowly but surely bringing it down to a nice steady trot in whatever direction you want to go.

Affirmations to encourage the light

Repeat the following affirmations first thing in the morning as you wake or last thing at night before you go to sleep to enhance and invite light to come into your life. You can also print these off together or cut them out individually to stick around various significant places in your home in order for your subconscious to pick up on these whenever they come into your focused or peripheral vision.

- *I am a magnet for positivity and attract enlightening situations to brighten my world.*
- *Everyone I meet feels my light radiating out towards them and my energy positively affects people for their highest good.*
- *My mind and body is in balance and harmony, encouraging growth through meaningful experience.*
- *I am a conduit for light and my life has purpose, order and I am free.*
- *I attract light in all ways to enhance, heal and honour my life for the greater good.*

Your light bulb moment

When I was a little girl I could sense when my angels visited me and, on a few occasions, saw them in my bedroom at night as these huge, transparent light eruptions, which startled me at first! Never wanting to scare or drive them away, I explained to them that sometimes this form overwhelmed me and I asked if they could come to me in a subtler, more gentle way. 'Of course Amanda, we only come to you with unconditional love and want you to feel safe and comforted by our messages.' From then on they appeared to me as orbs, soft glowing bulbs of light that appeared whenever I talked to my angels or asked for their help.

When you first start to connect with your angels they may take shape as something that does not complement your mood at the time or your personality more generally. Don't be afraid of them or feel cross with them! Relax, be patient and remember that you are only just getting to know one another. Tell them how you'd like to receive them and they will work with you and present themselves as you desire.

Use this exercise to tell your angels of light how they should appear to you, so you can relate to each other better.

Please write two lists:

(I) A list of symbols and/or forms of lights that overwhelm you.

(II) A list of symbols/forms of light that comfort you.

For example, in list (I) you might include strobe lights, mobile phones, televisions, lasers, etc. Under list (II) you might put sunlight, candles, prisms of light, orbs, etc. (Please note, there is no wrong answer here — be honest with yourself and write down whatever feels right for you.)

Now you have a clear idea about the forms of light that comfort you most, look out for them and, when they appear to you, it could mean that your angels are trying to tell you something. Revisit this exercise as often as you need to at first so that your angels of light can sympathise with your emotional state and alter their form with your daily experiences.

Chapter summary

So, what have you learned in this chapter to enable you to talk with your angels of light? Finding the light is not about seeking what isn't there, it's about uncovering and discovering what has always been. Understanding humanity's relationship with light from the beginning of time and how it's weaved into the very fabric of our existence physically, through belief and rituals and through the way we communicate with ourselves and others, will help you to become more empowered. Igniting your own light opens the door of communication with your angels and establishes rules of engagement with compassion for yourself. This builds mutual appreciation which deepens and develops that relationship further.

COUNT YOUR BLESSINGS

Why do you feel blessed today?...

2

Listen To Your Angels of Light

In times of need and anguish
You're there to help me rise.
A feather lands right next to me
An angel in disguise.

The Language of the Universe is a series of random but meaningful events that have no tangible explanation for their cause. You might think I mean coincidences, but I don't. This is something more special than that – messages from your angels of light.

The Language of the Universe can be confusing and overwhelming. Often this is because it reveals the truth, and the truth can hurt!

My life used to be riddled with misinterpretations of the Language of the Universe; much like woodworm, once it set in, the infestation was there to stay. Even though it took me some time to read the signs, it took me many years to trust the Language of the Universe to really let go and pay attention, much to the frustration of myself, let alone my loved ones. My angels' patience however was endless and they would often say to me *'Amanda, we are always here to help you if you're willing to receive.'*

Some would call it falling asleep. It's a term used when we're going about our day recognising some of the signs one moment and then oblivious to them the next or just switching down altogether. It is like walking around in a wakeful sleep. Even though I got the signs from my angels sometimes, I did not pay close enough attention regularly enough to avoid some seriously tricky, near life-threatening situations.

Finally, when I asked them in a meditation to help me learn, they appeared to me on the mental screen of my mind as a kaleidoscope of colours — blues, purples and pinks — merging and changing shape in brilliant and spectacular forms as they spoke and said:

'Amanda, awareness is key in enabling you to recognise the signs when they appear. Rather than dismiss what we know you see through fear or ignorance, accept them with grace and wait to see the message unfold if it's not already there for you. Lessons reveal themselves when the time is right.'

This was an invaluable lesson for me to learn at that time as I started to then take responsibility for paying attention rather than expecting them to make it obvious for me. I learned that I had to work on myself to become more aware, rather than rely on them to make even more effort to get my attention. Angels always help but equally we need to help ourselves. This chapter will show you how to pay better attention — to listen carefully to your angels of light.

Encouraging the signs

- **Prayer** — or conversing with your angels of light — is much like a telephone. It's your ability to call home every day or as much as you desire, so when you get entangled with your problems let the Universe untangle that knot of worries. It is your birthright to ask for help and your ability to be in alignment that helps you to receive the signs in answer to your prayers.

- **Dreams** — Remember to pay close attention to your dreams. Be particularly mindful of those that you remember or that linger with you throughout your day. It would be useful to have a journal next to your bed, or a dream diary, to record them as reading them back can relay many clues as to what message your angels are conveying to you through your subconscious mind. When we sleep at night we return to the consciousness where our blueprint is stored. Sometimes our day state is too chaotic for our logical mind to allow our messages to filter through, so our dreams are often a fountain of knowledge while we sleep.

- **Meditation** allows us to go inward in the present moment to disconnect from the physical world and allows us to focus on something particular, such as the breath, and to go into a tranquil state of mind. It's through developing the still and quiet moments that we can best develop clearer communication with our angels of light.

- **Yoga, t'ai chi and other similar practices** also allow us to become our inner witness. They also develop our core to open to our 'inner power'. The Sanskrit word for witness is *'sakshi'* (saa-kshe). *'Sa'* means 'with' and *'aksha'* means 'senses or eyes'. Becoming our own 'inner witness' through spiritual practice allows for us to deepen the inner senses and heighten our soul's growth.

- **Visualisation**, like meditation, allows for you to focus on specific images in your mind to heighten your senses. Practising this daily can deepen your relationship with your angels of light. By conjuring up a richness of colour, sounds, smell, tastes and feelings to amplify the pictures in your mind, you can develop all the inner senses more so in order to best interpret your angel messages.

- Spending time alone in **reflection** allows us to heighten our senses also. Sitting alone with a lit candle, using crystals to focus inwardly and being still, allows for your angels of light to communicate clearly with you while the outer senses step out of the way.

- **Keeping a journal or diary** is a great way to start recording your experiences while you explore your journey. I've kept a diary and journal since I was three years old which has been invaluable to me when recording dreams, thoughts and situations that I felt compelled to write about which later revealed vital insight. Downloading on to paper likewise allows our mind to declutter to allow our angel messages to come through loud and clear.

- **Mindfulness** — Paying attention to the body language of yourself and others can reveal so much information too. Your angels of light encourage you to become more mindful of reading situations, your surroundings and people, so eventually your ability increases to intuit the messages more accurately. Mindfulness originated in Eastern meditation practices to help pay attention in the present moment, with purpose and without judgement. The intention is to bring your attention to the present experience, moment by moment, so as to be fully immersed in the best possible place, thus reading what is going on in the here and now. This is where your power lies.

- **Energy management** — You are a high vibrational being that lives and interacts in a biosphere full of different vibrations, so feed your energy with spending time in nature to enhance and keep your energy field balanced. A healthy energy field produces a healthy body and environment. Likewise, beautifying your home and work surroundings feeds your energy field as the Universe and your angels of light love order. Look at your surroundings for clues as to what is going on within you. If you don't like the life you are living now, look at the signs. If you have broken, soiled and stained things in your life then

31

replace, repair and clean to reflect who you are aiming to be, not who you were.

- **Dedication to practice** – The more you incorporate spiritual regimes into your daily life, the easier it will be to understand the language your angels of light are conveying to you. You are given everything you need, so honour it. Think for the long term as it does take effort and dedication to start with, but it all comes down to the mind first and eventually it will come to you with ease.

- **Visions** – Signs come in all ways. We've spoken about dreams, but we can also have visions during our wake state. Our angels of light are responding to us always, so pay attention and write these down as soon as you observe them. Carry a pen and paper around with you if you feel you may forget to write them down later.

Recognising the signs

- **Orbs** are common to many as these particles of light are often seen in our peripheral vision in situations when our angels of light want us to know their presence. Paying attention to the different situations and when the orbs appear, gives us an understanding of what they're trying to communicate to us. I often see orbs around my clients when I'm talking about my angels, as a way for them to show me they are there when I need their reassurance.

- **Smells** are common too, but much harder to interpret as they come and linger only for a few seconds normally. When I smell cigarette smoke, despite no one around me smoking, I know it's a sign from my angels of light that my grandfather is with me. When I smell toast, it's my grandmother, and when I smell floral smells of any kind, despite there not being any logical reason for it, it's usually my angels just letting me know they're there.

- One of the most traditional and common ways for angels to show us signs is for us to find a **feather**. *'Feathers appear when angels are near'* is a common saying. As a child, I collected all the feathers that I found in gratitude for my angel protection and still do today. In fact, a feather landed on my bedside table just last night before I wrote this and it's still there now as a reminder for me.

- Sometimes if you look up at the sky when pondering on a situation or asking for angelic help, you may see a symbol or shape that means something to you in the form of a **cloud**. I often see shapes and faces in wallpaper, cracks in the pavement, designs on flooring and fabric, etc. that allow me to see the meaning. Being open to receive enhances our ability to see them.

- **Numbers** have symbolic meaning too. When I was a child I would repeatedly see the number 11 and still do today.

Often, I'll look at a digital clock after asking for my angels to help me and see it's 11.11. When I see this, I trust they have what I need in hand. Numbers are personal, so could include dates of birth, anniversaries or lucky numbers which have meaning to you and repeatedly appear in your life. What's your significant number?

- Seeing **letters** is very similar. I often see my initials or letters which represent messages on car registration plates. I had a client who was a police officer who constantly saw messages in car registration numbers which were very meaningful to him. If you keep seeing letters that are significant to you, write them down and see what your angels are trying to tell you.

- Sometimes we can experience a sudden **change in temperature** with no possible explanation, a sudden thought that prominently runs through our head which we cannot ignore, a message in a **lyric of a song** on the radio that has significance at that time or just that **compelling feeling you are not alone.** Whatever your experience is, accept it with non-judgement, gratitude and grace and be open to interpreting the message your angels of light are trying to convey to you. Often, they are just letting you know they are with you and sometimes it can be a message of specific importance. Discerning what feels right for you comes with practice.

- Many people feel a **tingling sensation** on the crown of the head when their angels are with them and some feel tingling in other areas of their body when they're healing themselves or helping others to heal. The tingling sensation is energy and I've found this to be one of my most profound communications from my angels of light over the years as it's the most tangible for me.

The Universe works with energy laws just as we work with laws that govern humanity. Our angels of light cannot beat us over the head to force us to see what is good for us — imagine! They exist to present us with clues that lead us to safety, closure or peace.

Back in the early days of my spiritual awakening and new-found fascination with the energy world, my angels guided me often by saying 'Read and absorb the message Amanda!' On one occasion I came across The Celestine Prophecy by James Redfield and was captivated by what he wrote about in relation to the experience of synchronicity and the 'unseen world'. This is when I started to make sense of the 'signs' which he highlights in his book and realised that my angels had guided me to read this in order to understand that we all have the ability to tap into the Language of the Universe.

At that time, I already knew a bit about synchronicity, but had no idea that we were all connected to that matrix. The concept is often traced back to a Swiss psychologist and psychoanalyst named Carl Jung, although some people argue that it was around for centuries before he introduced it to a wider audience. Jung used the term synchronicity or *'meaningful experience'* to describe his theory about how we all have the ability to experience these significant coincidences through *'a governing dynamic that underlays the whole of human experience'*.

Developing your auditory senses to listen to your angels of light

One of my clients has no visual conception whatsoever, which is known as congenital aphantasia, or mind blindness: he cannot use his imagination in the way we can. He worked in finance, in a very stressful job and, following burnout and constant injuries and ill health, he turned to holistic healing when all other methods to compensate for his life-style had failed him. As his health improved, he started to become aware that at the core of his being he wanted to help others, so he joined a local healing group which led him to discover his flourishing interest in mediumship.

He started coming to my regular monthly development group shortly after, as he wanted to find a way of communicating with his angels and enhance what he was discovering about himself. I realised that he had strong auditory senses, so when he got a little frustrated with not 'seeing' like the rest of the group, I recommended he worked with me on a one-to-one basis.

My angels and I looked at how his lifestyle was still inhibiting him and they responded with *'Robert loves structure in his life, so give him practices that will serve his highest good.'* So I set him rituals that included meditation, affirmations, walking in nature and working with talismans and crystals to counterbalance the negative impact his work was having on him. He placed crystals in his environment to absorb the negative energy that he was subjecting himself to and carrying back into his home. He started to incorporate ten minutes of meditation into his day before he got up to go to work and read positive affirmations which encouraged his growth and wellbeing before he slept at night.

Slowly but surely, he became aware of his angels talking to him as the external concerns and the internal noise chatter reduced enough for him to hear them. This created a surprising life change for him. He was still able to continue with his job, no longer challenged by the demands of others, but his angels encouraged him to set up his own healing group which he runs today. He finally found his 'tribe' and has become surrounded by loving, compassionate and well-meaning people and continues to build respect from his growing community.

Today, he conveys messages through his angels from loved ones to comfort those in need and his life has found the richness and balance that has helped illuminate the true essence of his passion to help others, counterbalancing the daily ordeal his job once created for him.

Meditation to connect with your angels of light

This is a meditation that can be used to ask your angels of light for a vision, statement or feeling that will lead you to a meaningful light bulb moment. Think of meditation as opening a metaphysical door from the physical world into the energy world every time you want to communicate with your angels. Using your own personal 'key' from then on can be used to symbolically invite them in to communicate with you whenever you wish.

By incorporating meditation into your daily life, it will help you become whole and aligned to your authentic self as you stimulate your own body's natural healing for mental, physical, emotional and spiritual wellbeing. As your stress levels reduce, the internal and external sounds lessen so you can enhance your life and match the new lighter vibration, creating better communication with your angels of light.

To find your own personal symbol, first set your intentions by going out to somewhere in nature perhaps, where you won't be disturbed. Finding your own personal place away from people, manmade structures and noise, in as natural a setting as possible, will help you connect deeper. If you can't go out into nature, find a quiet room in your home which you feel sets a tranquil scene. I encourage you to try this meditation away from electrical appliances such as televisions, computers and phones. Instead light a candle for your intention to receive light.

If you wish, you can record this meditation slowly, so that you can play it to yourself whenever you wish to communicate with your angels. Your intention here is to receive your symbol. If you wish to go on and use this meditation as part of your daily routine, then you can simply focus on that symbol at the appropriate part of the meditation and be mindful of what your angels are conveying to you.

Find a comfortable place to sit (as opposed to lying down), close your eyes and let yourself become aware of your breath. Focusing on the breath, begin to count to four slowly as you breathe in, and then count to four slowly again as you breathe out. Continue focusing on your breath for about a minute, or however long feels right and good for you.

While focusing on your breath, scan your body from your head to your toes, relaxing every inch of your physical being. Start moving your focus from the top of your skull to your forehead, eyes, ears, nose, cheeks, chin, throat and the whole of your neck and shoulders. As you scan through each part of your body you're telling each part to gently *relax, relax, relax.*

Moving down your body to your chest, arms, hands, fingers, stomach, lower abdomen, upper back, lower back, pelvis and hips, let your whole self unwind, focusing on the inside of your body as well as the outside.

Moving further down to your thighs, knees, calves and shins, ankles, feet and toes, tell your whole body that you are now completely tranquil and calm. You should be feeling in a peaceful state, physically, mentally and spiritually.

You are now calm and in a deeply restful state. Every time you do this exercise, you'll become more and more relaxed going deeper and deeper every time.

Let us begin.

Imagine you are in a beautiful garden, sitting on a bench under the shade of a tree with the sun just warm enough on your skin to make you feel serene and comfortable. The birds are singing in the trees, squirrels are playfully chasing one another on the branches, you can hear the calming waters running behind you in a narrow stream and all around you is a natural meadow of grass full of flowers moving gracefully like a gentle dance in the warm afternoon breeze.

The bench that you're sitting on is in front of a narrow footpath that weaves through the meadow and you now get up and start to walk slowly along that footpath, feeling the warm sun energising and rejuvenating your body. You feel deeply contented and nurtured by your surroundings.

You walk for a while, feeling the knee-high grass gently touching your lower legs until you finally come to the edge of the meadow and find yourself at a bricked wall with a wooden door directly in front of you. You have a key in your pocket. You take it out and place the key into the lock and turn it slowly. You twist the large metal doorknob and the door opens with ease. As you move through the door you walk into a walled garden full of beautiful flowers and you know that you are going to receive an important image or message from your angels.

Shut the door behind you so it is only you and your angels and wait until you receive your symbol of connection from them. Be patient and trust that you will receive your symbol if it does not appear instantly. When you are ready you may receive a vision of a scene, a person or an object that will mean something significant to you. Don't worry if you cannot work out the significance of the vision that comes to you, simply continue to relax, don't judge yourself or your angels and the meaning will eventually come to you naturally.

When you get something that you feel is symbolic allow your senses to heighten that symbol. Absorb how you feel in this moment. Let every sensation sit with you. Can you hear any sounds? Is anyone talking to you or are you running your own thoughts about your symbol? Again, let everything sit with you a while longer. Can you smell anything in relation to your symbol or surroundings? If you can, then breathe it in to every cell of your body and let that sit with you for a while too. And finally, if you feel compelled to touch your symbol or something in relation to it, reach out and allow your hands to explore it respectfully.

When you feel you have absorbed all the sensations available to you in this moment, thank your angels for giving you your symbol and tell them that you will use it with love and gratitude every time you wish to communicate with them in the future. Now turn around, walk back through the door and lock it with the key.

Slowly walk back to your bench at the end of the meadow, being mindful of how you feel now you have

41

received your symbol. Do you feel different? Do you feel lighter perhaps? Have you received a message that you're taking with you that will change your life in some way? Whatever you notice, observe it without judgement, with kindness and love, knowing that your life has been touched by your angels and that when you take it back into your physical world you will keep it locked deep inside you to help you on your journey through life.

When you finally get back to the bench, sit down and take in the beautiful scene all around you, absorbing the warmth of the sun, the glory of the surrounding natural environment, the sounds of the animals and birds that play among the trees, smell the richness of the soil, the trees and the flowers and absorb the calm and peace.

When you feel ready, plant your feet firmly on the ground, earthing yourself back to reality. Be reassured in the knowledge that you are returning to the quiet space you created for yourself before entering the meditation.

Whenever it feels right and good for you, open your eyes and come back fully.

From now on, whenever you wish to communicate with your angels, you can use this meditation as part of your spiritual practice once a day, once a week or whenever you feel the urge. To enhance your messages and to deepen your spiritual journey, incorporating this as often as you can will enhance your awareness as it awakens the inner senses.

If you are time-poor or need to communicate with your angels for help when under pressure, then simply find a quiet space, close your eyes, focus on deep breathing, counting in and out for four seconds for a minute, and then project your symbol into your mind. Ask your angels to guide and assist you in any way you need at that time. When you connect with them, receive a message from them or feel you will receive it when the time is right, thank them and know that all will be well and open your eyes.

Meditation is a beautiful way to start building a long and meaningful relationship with your angels of light. However you decide to use this meditation, always remember that this is *your communication* with *your angels*, so please adapt it using methods that work best for you. While meditating you may receive more than one symbol at a time and that's OK too. My symbols are often heart-shaped or feathers.

I love receiving my symbols when I least expect them because it comforts me to know my angels are never far and always want to communicate with me.

Your light bulb moment

Recognising the signs takes practice. Today, I was putting the washing out in my garden when I heard a gurgling sound coming from a nearby overflow drain. I thought it was a blockage but, as I approached it, through the grill I saw a huge toad that was trapped and looking back at me. I took the drain cover off and helped him out. Living right next to the park, I set off to release him into the open space for safety. At that exact moment a woman walked up to me and asked what I was doing. When I explained she said: *'That's incredible They're endangered. What a lucky toad. I hope he rewards you well!'*

It was when I got back into the house, my angels reminded me of the story of toads and diamonds which was my favourite fairy story as a child. The story was that a young girl came upon an old crone in the woods and, when asked, gave her the only food she had. To her surprise she was granted the gift of diamonds coming out of her mouth every time she spoke from then on. When her jealous sister discovered her good fortune, she set off into the woods looking for the old crone but came across a beautiful woman who asked for some food. *'Absolutely not,'* she said, *'I'm saving this for someone else.'*

As she started to walk away, the beautiful young woman changed into the old crone and granted her the gift of toads coming out of her mouth every time she spoke from then on.

Seeing this 'sign' for what it is and being reminded by my angels of this story, came at exactly the right time as I was writing this, of the invaluable lesson of non-judgement. When we walk through life without expectation but are open to the signs, then true magic happens!

Choose either a symbol that your angels of light may have given you in your meditation or something significant such as a butterfly, bee, something relevant that someone will say to you today, or perhaps a song that plays on the radio that has a deep message for you, etc. Then ask your angels of light to show you this sign within the next forty-eight hours. When it appears, record it and spend a few moments reflecting what message your angels of light are revealing to you.

Chapter summary

So, what have you learned in this chapter to enable you to talk with your angels of light? The Language of the Universe is woven into the very fabric or your everyday experience. Rituals and non-judgement encourage recognition of these signs and help them to come to the forefront of your awareness. Signs are the conduit between yourself and your angels of light to clarify you are exactly where you should be in life, to provide evidence of their existence, to teach you invaluable lessons or provide solutions to whatever you are asking for help with.

COUNT YOUR BLESSINGS

Why do you feel blessed today ?...

....

....

....

....

....

....

....

....

....

....

....

....

....

....

....

....

....

....

....

3

Look for Your Angels of Light

I dream a life inside my head
A sea of fantasy,
And while I sleep, you carve and make
My life as ecstasy.

Angels' appearances and visualisation

Every one of us is unique so it's not surprising that our angels will appear to us in various ways. Some see huge apparitions with mighty wings, some see playful cherubs and others still may see nothing at all and yet may feel or hear them whisper wisdom. Depending on what our path is, how it best serves us, angels of light will appear in the form that we best understand.

When I was a child, my angels came to me in such a powerful form that at times it frightened me! In my dreams, I could hear them talk to me as clearly as the adults around me in my waking day, calling out to me *'Amanda, come and play with us'* but their appearances were like nothing I'd ever experienced before. They were transparent wisps of unfurling light, with hues of colour — so subtle, yet so mesmerising. When they flew with me they changed shape playfully, tantalising my young and developing imagination.

On many occasions, they still appear in my dreams in a human form, taking on the persona or characteristics of a person they wish to portray. They whisper to me when I'm quiet and alone during the day, cry out to me when I'm busy or not listening, and when I'm communicating with people and they want me to pay attention to what we're discussing, they'll often appear as different coloured light orbs around the person I'm talking to.

I've learned over the years that different colours mean different things. Blue orbs tell me that the person I'm with needs to communicate something or I need to listen to them. Purple indicates they are on a strong spiritual journey and pink alerts me to them having relationship difficulties or a need to open their heart.

Dreams

My angels appeared in my dreams as a multitude of coloured light beings, constantly shifting and changing shape and form. They were ever metamorphosing. Like swirls of coloured paint, one minute they were silhouettes, the next they became human-like with flowing locks of golden or auburn hair. They twisted and turned into different creative structures to fill my stories. Whatever my dream was, their presence was always unconditionally loving. During my waking state, it spooked me at such a young age to see those colours merging and manifesting, so I prayed for them to show their presence in a more acceptable form for me to deal with. And they did, responding to me with *'Amanda we are always here to serve your highest good!'* From then on they always appeared to me in a way that reassured, rather than startled me.

Instead of huge forms, they appeared as tiny flickering orbs when they needed to show me they were there. My body became a barometer and I started to experience tingles, felt pressure touches or a sudden change in temperature as I sensed their presence, and their voices came through gently but clearly as if they were standing beside me in the room.

Simon came to see me when he worked as a police officer. The love of his life had left him shortly after he had an accident at work which had left him with long-term physical damage. He became depressed, was broken and struggled to keep going in his job. He was also struggling to cope financially. His world seemed to be folding in on him.

At the time he visited me, he was having dreams in which it seemed angels were trying to help him. He'd also started to become aware of repetitious signs during his daily life which seemed to indicate that they were there with him. He didn't understand the dreams nor what the signs meant, so he asked me to help.

I encouraged Simon to speak every night to his angels, just before he went to sleep, to see why they were helping him. I told him to simply ask: *'Angels of light, please help me to learn how to communicate with you better and to clearly understand the messages that you are sending me in my dreams and my wake state. Thank you, with love and gratitude.'*

I then asked him to record his dreams.

By encouraging Simon to look at what he'd detailed while he was in a relaxed state, and to examine it from a symbolic viewpoint, it gave him the confidence to gradually interpret what his angels were saying to him. Likewise, during his day, whenever he saw a sign which he felt held a significant message, he noted it down. Later, when he was in bed and in a relaxed state, he would ask his angels what the sign meant. Sometimes his angels were able to show him through the mental screen of his mind what the sign meant; on other occasions, the meaning would come to him in the form of a dream. The more Simon worked in this way, the deeper his understanding became. This resulted in him seeing changes in his life.

Simply using that optimum time when our mind is at the right frequency to connect with our angels, enables our messages and requests to get through and for us to hear or see what our angels are trying to communicate with us.

After working on this for a few weeks, Simon was called to a hospital as the first police officer to tend to the victim of a horrific acid attack. This had a life-changing impact on him and, for the first time, he experienced an awareness of a whole new level of compassion and emotions towards this victim which he'd not experienced with others before, and so began an unfolding of huge lessons in valuing human life.

This was a turning point for Simon. Continuing to talk to his angels who constantly guided him through signs and messages in his dreams, Simon eventually settled down with a beautiful new partner, deepened his relationships with his friends and family members and left the job that no longer served him. Starting up his own business proved successful, not only because it allowed him to live out a role which was more aligned with his growing spiritual beliefs, but it also supported his long-term injury as he finally received a significant compensatory pay out, which enabled him to invest in his health and wellbeing and his new unfolding future.

Simon believed that if he'd continued working as a policeman as his mental wellbeing declined, he may have reached the stage where suicide seemed the only option. Instead, today he lives an inspiring and active life, talking with his angels, who guide him in all ways to improve his life and the lives of those around him.

Paying attention to our emotions, positive but especially negative emotions, is key to giving us insight we may otherwise overlook. Sometimes it isn't clear at the time why we may be experiencing something but becoming aware of it with non judgement may allow us to receive answers when the time is right. For example, a few days ago, I was having a beautiful day with my partner, having just visited an art gallery, and we were driving to a particular location for lunch, when I suddenly experienced a deep feeling of grief and rejection. Because I was talking with my partner, I couldn't easily tune in and ask my angels what it meant at the time, but it left an impression on me and I knew I had to find out what the feeling meant.

The following day, I was with my yogini (a female master practitioner of yoga) for our weekly session and during a meditation, where she was chanting, I had a profound experience. About halfway through, I could smell burning rubber and thought there was a fire. Suddenly I was anxious about her two small children who I knew were upstairs in her house, while also wondering how we would all get out of the building. Eventually the smell and my concern went and I relaxed back into the meditation.

When she'd finished, and before I could say anything, she told me that she'd been chanting the *Pavamana Suktam*, a famous chant from the Vedic tradition, which burns away and purifies past traumas. At that moment my angels appeared and whispered *'Amanda, pay attention to what we are showing you'* and showed me a vision in the form of a memory from ten years earlier: I'd been walking with my children early before school one morning and we came across a house fire. It was rare for us to go out so early and there was no one else around. I settled my children some-where safe and ran to the house, climbed on to some bins in the garden and in through a kitchen window. I managed to rescue two small children and a dog from the burning house. That house was filled with black acrid smoke from burning rubber.

My angels showed me that I never hesitated that day ten years ago and had had no fear going into such a serious and dangerous situation. They then contrasted this with me two days earlier when I had felt both grief and rejection. The area I had driven through with my partner had brought to mind a memory of a close friend who used to live there, who'd once rejected me. The angels showed me that my feelings were a reminder of a pattern I'd held on to since early childhood.

Looking back, I reflected that throughout my life I'd gone into new situations with a fear of rejection which had often created exactly that, or worse. This also explained why I once had a huge fear of public speaking. My angel's message was clear:

'Amanda, you are now embarking on new experiences which may sometimes bring up old fears. It is human nature. Every experience is unique and going into them with an open heart and a curious mind will continue to allow you to grow as you create new positive memories. As these new memories form, they will compact the old negative memories down to the recesses of your mind, as they no longer serve you. Your new memories will take over and encourage growth for your highest good.'

I'm very grateful to my angels of light for constantly teaching me such lessons for growth and comfort, in their loving support. Our angels are always trying to get our attention but it is up to us to learn how to talk with them if we want to enhance our lives for the better.

A visualisation meditation

This is an incredibly relaxing meditation and certainly helps those who find it difficult to quieten the mind chatter or keep focused on guided meditations. It's also incredibly healing. To deepen your visualisation, using chants, relaxation or classical music can not only cleanse and heal past traumas, but can clear a space for heightened awareness and clearer communication with your angels of light.

You could, for example, download the *Pavamana Suktam* from the Internet (it's about eight minutes long) or find some music that resonates with you. I listen to whatever I feel drawn to at any given time and have amassed a varied collection of music over the years, playing with different tones and rhythms for different effects. Experiment and see what calls you. Once you start listening to something that you've chosen, you will often find that it will take you on a deeper and deeper journey every time you hear it.

Find a time of day that works best for you. I do this in the morning before I start my day, when there's little distraction. Make sure any phones are switched off, find a comfortable place to sit — if possible sit with your feet planted on the floor and your hands in your lap, face up (in order to receive guidance from your angels). I also have my journal to hand to write down any messages from my angels. It would be an ideal time for you to start practising this yourself. Now . . .

Close your eyes and listen to your chosen music for at least ten minutes. Allow your breathing to slow to a steady rhythm. Don't worry if thoughts come into your mind. Observe them and let them drift away like clouds in the sky. Be mindful of what you see, whether it be colours, shapes, visions, memories; whatever you observe, just view it with curiosity. When the music has finished or you're ready to come back into the room, gently open your eyes, letting the colours blend back into focus. Take your journal and make any notes that you feel inspired to write.

There is no right or wrong way of doing this as every experience will be different, but doing this exercise regularly will enhance your visualisation technique and deepen your communication with your angels of light.

Your light bulb moment

Dreams are our way of interpreting what our angels are communicating to us through our subconscious. You have the ability to decipher your own dreams and signs when relaxed. I started a dream journal several years ago when I first recognised that my angels were speaking to me in my dreams as I had been too busy to pick up their signs during the day. I still, all these years later, have one in my bedside drawer. Try the following exercise to see what messages your angels are communicating to you.

For the next seven days, keep your journal with you during the day and keep it by your bedside at night. Before you go to sleep, with your eyes closed and sitting up in bed, ask your angels the following:

'Angels of light, please help me to learn how to communicate with you better and to clearly understand the messages that you are sending me in my dreams and my wake state. Thank you, with love and gratitude.'

Then go to sleep.

As you wake each day from your dream state, try to keep your eyes closed and reinforce what you can remember from any dreams you may have had. It may well be the last one that you had just before waking. Do not worry if you can't do this at first. Keep practising each morning, with no judgement, and stay as relaxed as you possibly can so you fully absorb the dream. At this stage, do not try to analyse it. As soon as you open your eyes, record it in your journal. As you're still in a relaxed mode, ask your angels to help you to understand the message. If you do, record it in your journal, too. If you don't, then just be patient and try again the next night. The more you practise, the better you'll become at this.

Chapter summary

So, what have you learned in this chapter to enable you to talk with your angels of light? Your angelic experience will be totally unique to you, depending on what works for your highest good and blends with your life experience. Your dream state is your subconscious playground, so becoming adept at remembering and recording your dreams encourages your angelic communication and will enhance your mind to recognise signs during your wake state. Regular visualisation meditation will increase your ability to decipher signs that your angels of light are encouraging you to see.

COUNT YOUR BLESSINGS

Why do you feel blessed today?...

....

....

....

....

....

....

....

....

....

....

....

....

....

....

....

....

....

....

....

4

The Inner Senses

Shades of blue, orbs of light
A song I call my own.
And as I feel your warm embrace
You always guide me home.

Dr Joseph Banks Rhine studied the phenomena of parapsy-chology (the study of mental phenomena which are excluded from or inexplicable by orthodox scientific psychology) at Duke University in Durham, North Carolina, where he and his wife, Dr Louisa Rhine, created the term extrasensory perception or ESP. From the 1930s, Banks discovered that, apart from the physical senses, there were also three inner senses which enabled people to garner information.

At first the Rhines' experiments were focused on mediums only, to establish evidence of an afterlife, in order that they might establish that they were using senses beyond our accepted physical senses. Joseph Rhine then started experi-menting with students in laboratory conditions using specially designed cards with symbols on, asking them to predict what was on the cards without them having seen them. Later he went on to use dice and created a dice machine to see if students could influence the outcome of the throw of the dice. The Rhine Research Center still continues today to advance and explore consciousness and the inner senses of the human experience.

The inner senses

Our five outer senses are, of course, our ability to see, hear, touch, smell and taste.

Our three inner senses are:

1. Clairvoyance — our ability to see on the mental screen of our mind.

2. Clairaudience — the ability to hear communication from the energy world.

3. Clairsentience — the ability to feel or intuit.

The three inner senses are important features of our spiritual make-up.

Fostering your own inner faculties will offer a wonderful new means of communicating with your angels of light, which in turn will bring many benefits to your overall health and wellbeing. Some people can tune into their three inner senses from the moment they are born, but it does not matter if you have little or even no experience of using your inner senses yet. We all have the ability to use these three senses and this chapter will show you how you can begin.

I developed clairaudience, the ability to hear communication from the energy world, at a young age to avoid anxiety-inducing situations. An example of this was as a child I had to set an alarm clock to wake up in the morning, but I was extremely anxious about waking up my younger brother and getting told off. I had no reason to be worried for long because my angels reassured me with '*Amanda, we will help and wake you when you need us to*' and set a timer that rang loudly in my subconscious mind exactly one minute before the actual alarm was due to ring each morning. This meant that I could wake up without stirring my sleeping brother and so avoid being scolded.

I developed my clairsentience faculty, the ability to feel or intuit, as a child. My father had a menagerie of animals which I loved so much, I knew instinctively if they were sick or suffering. I had an amazing empathy towards them that meant that I knew I could heal them.

The first time I experienced this was when I was about six and I'd come home from school one day to discover a sick lop-eared rabbit, lying panting on her side. As I'd spent many years playing with and establishing a special kinship with the animals, I reached out, scooped her up and sat down on the grass, laying her across my lap. As I was stroking her, I could feel tingling in my hands and hear my angels of light saying, *'Just gently lay your hands on her stomach Amanda.'* I did that for some time.

An extraordinary calm came over us both, like we were cocooned and detached from our surroundings. I felt so much love at that moment for that rabbit and it was as if she knew it and trusted that I was trying to help her and then I heard my angels say *'When you give love unconditionally Amanda, you will receive this back in life in many ways.'* The next morning when I went to see her in the rabbit pen, she was hopping about and playing with all the other rabbits. From then on, without question, whenever I found a sick animal, I felt an empathy towards helping them and often did. It was a lesson in giving and receiving love that continues to teach me today. I never recall my father calling a vet in except for when my dog got knocked down by a car and needed surgery. Healing seemed to be a very instinctive and natural thing for me to do as a child, although it took me many years to accept that as an adult and to use this to help in other ways.

The frequencies of the mind

It's important to develop a more alpha-based frequency of the mind to sharpen your three inner senses and this assures you that the insight you receive can be trusted. There are four different frequencies that are triggered through high-to-low activity:

1. Beta — This is when the mind is strongly engaged in active conversation, stressful situations or worry. You activate beta in fight or flight, such as when running for a bus. Being in a beta state of mind for long periods of time can lead to heightened states of anxiety, ill health and imbalances in your life.

2. Alpha — This is a rejuvenating and relaxing state, often experienced during the day when you take time out. It's also experienced as you start to daydream, meditate and go into the early stages of sleep. Developing a more alpha-based mindset through activities which induce this frequency, stimulates the immune system promoting health and wellbeing and bridges the gap between our conscious thinking and subconscious mind. It promotes a relaxed state of mind, so that you're connected to Source and therefore can trust the information that comes through the inner senses.

3. Theta — This is a deeper form of relaxation experienced in deep hypnosis, meditation or the sleep state. It's when your mind activity is switched off and you have the ability to allow the subconscious to remove unwanted habits and to promote wellbeing. Your inner senses work through the more relaxed frequencies such as alpha and theta.

4. Delta — Finally, this is the deepest sleep state where you are completely relaxed physically and mentally.

To stimulate a more alpha-based mindset you need to create a calm and tranquil space for yourself daily by incorporating good practices into your daily routine. A great daily routine might look something like this:

First thing in the morning as you wake and before you get out of bed, sit up and, with your eyes closed and in a comfortable relaxed state, visualise a peaceful and tranquil scene, somewhere you love to go and meditate perhaps. You might see yourself on a beach or by a river. Wherever you go, let your senses bring in all the colours, sounds, smells, tastes perhaps, and feelings associated with that scene. Sit with it for five minutes before you open your eyes and start your day with the right 'frame or frequency' of mind which will open the doors to receive your angels of light's insight.

If you are trying to access the alpha-frequency mindset for the first time, then do not be despondent if it does not happen for you straight away. When I look back at my formative days, when I first committed to my own spiritual journey, I spent huge amounts of time and money attending workshops and hypnotherapy lessons, reading piles of books and travelling all over the world to sacred places. I could only control my inner senses intermittently and received psychic information in dribs and drabs. It seemed to me that everyone else in my workshop groups or the meditation classes I joined were able see huge, breathtaking visual images and hear great reels of conversation from their angels of light — it made me think that I was not as gifted as them! I urge you now to try to not feel disappointment if it takes you some time to develop your inner senses. The more pressure you put on yourself and your spiritual development, the more frustrated you will become with the process and the more you will slip into beta-frequency thinking and block your psychic channels.

Some years into my spiritual education I was nominated to appear as a contestant on a televised challenge for psychics. Despite my fears and reticence, my angels reassured me, when I asked them what I should do, with *'Amanda, this is your chance to stand in your truth. Take the challenge. The reward will be far more than you think.'* So, I decided to go on the programme to convey the important message that we all have psychic ability. During the competition, to my surprise, I got through the audition processes and pilot show to end up as one of the finalists on the main programme. I learned an invaluable lesson, which I will share with you now.

On the first day of filming, the television company asked me to come to London so I could be driven to a secret location where the first challenge would take place. I was really nervous because I had a fear of public speaking back then and so was extremely anxious en route. I had not eaten all day and had to wait in a strange hotel room for hours until I was finally taken to the secret location. I had an incredibly painful headache, was blindfolded and just wanted to go home because I was feeling so dreadful.

When we arrived at the location and my blindfold was removed, I found myself at a garage somewhere in the depths of south London. It was the end of an icy-cold, dark afternoon in December. A woman, the producer, arrived with a clipboard and headset and I opened my window from the back of the car, so she could speak to me.

She told me that I was the last contestant of the day, that hardly anyone had succeeded with the challenge and that I would have to *give it my all* as the crew had been there all day, were tired, cold and hungry and wanted to go home. I was being forced to hurry through my challenge as quickly as possible, which increased the pressure weighing down on my naïve shoulders. This put me into a heightened stressed state of emotion and I was therefore running constantly in the beta-frequency of my mind, which I didn't realise was disconnecting me from my angels – who I now needed more than ever if I was to succeed!

The challenge itself took place in a large covered car park filled with cars, crew, lights and cameras, all of which only added to my increasing anxiety. The female presenter welcomed me to the show and handed me an envelope containing my task: a photograph of a man whom I had to find, currently hiding in the boot of one of the fifty cars in the car park.

I was petrified but still trusted that my angels had got me to this stage for a reason. Still, as the enormity of the task dawned on me, my logical mind felt defeated and stressed. I took a deep sigh, feeling it was a lost cause from the onset, then to my utter surprise the inside of my mind was suddenly flooded with the colour navy blue (clairvoyance). I had sighed out of resignation, but in that moment that sigh had relaxed me enough to receive some insight from my angels, even though I then went back into anxiety mode again shortly after their first message.

I assumed through logical mind thinking that the man was in a navy blue car. As I looked around the car park there was not a single navy blue car that I was attracted to. I realised that I was following an assumption based on what my logical mind was telling me rather than what my inner senses knew to be true. This taught me to *never assume anything.*

I grew panicky again and prayed to my angels to help me. In my mind I cried out: *'Please angels, give me something to go on!'*

I did not seem to get any answers at first and gave another sigh just as I was about to give up again. Instantly, a bright yellow registration plate flashed into my mind with the capital letters 'C', 'U', 'R' on it. For a moment, I felt hopeful but then lapsed back into stress mode. Once again, I assumed through logical mind thinking that the registration plate I was looking for contained these three letters. I scanned the car park but found no such car.

I could feel the crew were getting restless; they did not believe in me and wanted to go home. I was so disappointed and yet in a desperate last-bid attempt to give it my best shot I started shouting at my angels in my head, pleading with them to help me.

'*Come on angels, what am I supposed to do now? They're about to stop recording if I don't pull this off!*'

I repeated the letters 'C', 'U', 'R' — until finally the penny dropped. This was my light bulb moment. It was as if I had to be pushed to my limits to finally realise, after repeating it several times, that they were not the letters of the registration plate but rather a code for '*see you are* the number plate' (clairaudience).

I quickly walked around the garage again to find a car with a number plate that related to me somehow. Sure enough, I spotted a white car with a registration number that matched my own initials. I walked towards the car and felt warmth radiating from a distance of about two metres away (clairsentience).

I can sometimes be a typically sceptical Capricorn and want a little more clarification of something, as in this case. I wanted to confirm that it was the right vehicle and so I asked my angels to send me something more to go on.

'*OK, so if this is the car angels, please show me how to know for sure,*' I said to them in my mind one last time.

Instantly, an image came into my mind showing me a hypnotherapy teacher who had taught me about using my body as a pendulum if I ever needed clarification of a 'Yes' or 'No' answer to something. I gave it a shot and sensed my body saying '*Yes*'. I asked the presenter to unlock the boot and, to my huge relief, a man dressed from head to toe in navy blue jumped out for all to see. I had done it!

That day taught me the importance of making decisions in the right frequency of the mind in order to receive messages from my angels. It taught me to trust in the process and to never assume anything using logical mind thinking. I received the colour navy blue from my angels right at the beginning of the task, which made me appreciate that sometimes the nuggets of insight we receive from our angels are not always in the order that we necessarily want them at first! I have used what I learned that day to complete numerous puzzles throughout my life since. That day my faithful angels showed me that I could succeed under pressure, I could conquer my anxiety and always improve my ability if I remain open to learning. I will always be grateful to my angels for helping me that day. They motivated me to dig deeper on my spiritual journey and spurred me on to help others unlock their own psychic abilities.

Kate came to me when she started to experience odd things happening in her home. Eventually it became apparent that her angels were trying to get her attention. Kate led an incredibly busy life in the pony racing world and loved to have healing sessions when she came to see me where she would lie in a deep state of relaxation and allow her mind to let go and her body to go into a tranquil and restorative state of being. During her sessions, she started to see images in her mind in quite graphic detail. When we interpreted them after, it was clear how her angels were conveying messages to help guide her through the many challenges she was facing in her life. Kate had multiple challenges which were putting considerable strain on herself, her family and business.

As she responded so well to the healing sessions, I encouraged her to incorporate simple five-minute or so visualisation meditations into her daily life, to stimulate a more alpha-based mindset. As Kate was an earthy woman, she loved the idea of using crystals which she intuitively bought herself to place in several rooms in her home. Soon, she noticed the change in the energy of her family members and the house took on a clearer, calmer and more ener-gised atmosphere. I also recommended that she use flower remedies which I chose intuitively for her to work with and balance her emotions.

Kate then started to remember her dreams more, recording them and her angel messages came to her clearer through signs in her daily life too as she started to develop her clair-voyance. As the internal noise chatter was turned down and her outer environment became more tranquil, she started to trust the messages she heard from her angels, which were becoming clearer to her as she developed her clairaudience.

By using the flower remedies and feeling herself and her family members healing, as she worked with horses, Kate's empathy with them deepened as she started to feel just what to do herself to help them when they became sick.

Kate's world is now full of opportunity for growth and her solutions to overcome challenges come to her clearly from her angels who guide her daily. She has embarked on a journey of learning about her natural healing and intuitive ability and often helps other people in the horse world who are facing many similar challenges. Kate was already a respected and accomplished horsewoman and seeing the changes she has since made for herself, her family and business has made her even more credible, attracting those to her that now seek her help in order to go through their own changes through her guidance and support.

Affirmations for enhancing your intuitive faculties and increasing your creativity

These affirmations will help you to identify areas of your life that are simply blocking your insight and creativity and therefore sabotaging the flow of communication with your angels. Remember, your angels can guide you wherever you want them to take you, but it's ultimately down to you to look out for and honour the images they show you. We often have creative blockages through fear.

Repeat the following first thing in the morning, as soon as you wake up, or last thing at night, when you're about to go to sleep, to enhance your spiritual growth.

- *I have clear-sightedness which enables me to see the signs through the mental screen of my mind, that my angels are showing me in my dreams and wakefulness.*
- *I have sharp hearing so that my auditory senses are always alerted to the messages my angels are communicating to me through my thoughts and external voices and sounds.*

- *My body is a powerful intuitive communicator and I am able to identify messages from my angels through the feelings and sensations my body is speaking to me.*

Your light bulb moment

This exercise will help you to ask your angels of light for 'Yes' or 'No' answers to give you confirmation when you need it most. Try this simple exercise to use your body as a pendulum when you're on your own which you can then use whenever you need it.

Stand upright in flat shoes or barefooted. Relax your body and clear your mind. When you feel nice and calm, take a few deep breaths and ask your angels of light: *'Which way will my body sway for "Yes"?'* Then sense if your body is swaying gently back and forth or from side to side. Once you've detected which way your body sways for 'Yes', you can then ask another question to which you know the answer to, such as, 'Is my mother's name Marianne?' If your mother's name is Carole, for example, then you should feel your body sway to indicate 'No'. Try this a few times if you wish for other questions that you know the answer to.

After a little bit of practise, ask a question you don't know the answer to. Record the answer in your journal and see what the outcome is. Each time you go back to this exercise, always ask your angels which way your body is set before you ask a question you need to know the answer to.

Try out this exercise with your friends. The more you practise, the more confidence you'll create in using this valuable exercise in the future.

Chapter summary

So, what have you learned in this chapter to enable you to talk with your angels of light? By working to develop and enhance your three inner senses, your clairvoyance, clairaudience and clairsentience, it connects you straight to the Divine enabling you to transmit and receive communication to and from your angels of light. Becoming mindful of when you are switched on to the right frequencies of your mind, enables you to accept the messages that you receive and to discern that they are coming from the angelic realm. Using techniques to become a more 'alpha'-based person ultimately improves your life in all ways which is what your angels of light are encouraging you to achieve.

COUNT YOUR BLESSINGS

Why do you feel blessed today?...

....
....
....
....
....
....
....
....
....
....
....
....
....
....
....
....
....
....

5

Alignment

Tumbling down my river path
An oar you give to steer.
You lead me to my resting place
To harmony from fear.

What is alignment?

Alignment is when we wake up in the morning and go through our day feeling at peace, feeling the joy of living, overcoming challenges and feeling the satisfaction and reward of resolution. It's when we attract all the right situations, people and solutions. I finally found that alignment through paying attention to what my angels of light were encouraging me to see so that I could make the necessary changes in my life.

The importance of alignment

The importance of aligning ourselves is therefore far more than just being in the right place at the right time for the things we want in life. When we align ourselves, we vibrate with the universal order to honour our mission here on earth: whether we are teachers, doctors, politicians, housewives or carers, we all have a vital role to play in this world.

When we align to play out the small part we're designed for among the seven-and-a-half billion people on our glorious planet, we impact on the greater whole to create a collective harmony and balance. We have a positive impact on the balance of the people around us, our environment and the world at large. It's like being a small piece of the jigsaw puzzle of life; once we slot into where we belong everything around us fits with precision and ease.

By aligning to our truth, it is not only when we face others that we honour this process, but when we face ourselves in the wee small hours when no one else is looking. Karma (the cycle of cause and effect) works twenty-four hours a day and, despite how we may feel we're projecting ourselves to the world, if we are not aligned to our truth, Karma plays out to give us the opportunity to right that course, if we so choose.

How does alignment help you to talk with your angels of light?

When we allow ourselves to align and become more balanced and in harmony with the essence of who we are, we heighten our communication with our angels and therefore to our purpose. We create the life we should be living as opposed to the struggle we think we had to endure in the past.

When we're in alignment, we're in exactly the right frequency to enable us to talk to our angels of light and for us to hear what they are saying, in turn. It's like a needle on a compass. If we allow ourselves to follow the right direction according to the instrument that's guiding us, i.e. our angels of light, then we end up where we should be.

The other night I had a ticket to go to a writers' event that had been recommended to me three weeks before while on a training course. As the weather was particularly hot and travelling on the Tube was going to be a feat in itself, I questioned whether I should bother going. It would have been a useful evening and yet I couldn't see the impact it would have on me by missing it. Before I left, I relaxed and asked my angels if I should go, to which they responded: *'Don't judge what you perceive this experience to be through your limited thinking, Amanda.'*

With my angels' encouragement, I realised that I needed to go — despite hitting the Tube during rush hour and arriving hot and dishevelled. I still questioned if I was in the right place as the only talk I was interested in was the last one of the evening. I was so tired, I didn't know if I'd even stay awake.

During the first session, a radio presenter walked into the room; I'd met him two days earlier at an event I'd been speaking at. He'd approached me after my talk to ask if he could interview me for his show; he had also recommended that I get in touch with a contact of his whom he felt would be beneficial to me. At the time, he'd written the person's name down on a piece of paper but I hadn't done anything about it yet.

I asked my angels whether I was still in the right alignment to be where I should be as I was so tired and at that stage had only seen the synchronicity of meeting the interviewer, but I wasn't yet quite getting the message.

They replied: *'Amanda, pay more attention and you'll see. Your weariness is distracting you and you're not quite in alignment.'*

With that, I stopped listening to the speaker and, taking a deep breath, relaxed. Suddenly the room faded out and the organiser of the event, who was sitting directly opposite me in front of a podium, seemed suddenly to be shrouded in a halo of light. Directly behind him was a banner, the letters seeming bolder than before. That's when the light bulb moment came and I saw the organiser's name and his company. It was the man I had been recommended to contact only two days before.

I was amazed as I'd booked the event weeks before I'd met the broadcaster, showing that I was in alignment and in the right place at the right time. Even though I was tired and distracted, as soon as I needed to talk to my angels of light, I took the right action to move myself into alignment, enabling myself to ask for and receive the insight from them necessary to clarify what I needed to know.

There are many reasons why we come out of alignment: distractions, dramas, trying to control where we think we need to be, and so on. By being mindful of why we've become unaligned and of getting back on to that 'right frequency', we become able to hear our angels clearly. Even when we are out of alignment, our angels will try to get our attention, but to truly communicate with them, we must make every effort to get on to that right frequency to fully understand the message. Being out of alignment is like getting some of the pieces to a jigsaw and not quite finishing it. We don't get to see the full picture.

How to achieve alignment and recognising imbalances

When we make the decision to embark on our spiritual journey or simply want to better our lives, it's important to first recognise what is going wrong. Identifying the imbalances in our everyday world encourages us to align with our true selves and become more mindful of our attitude and thoughts towards our existence.

At first it took me down what seemed a very long dark tunnel which I resigned myself to explore. You may have also felt like this yourself when you first embarked on your own personal spiritual quest for your truth — that feeling of being in that tunnel where you perhaps felt isolated, disconnected from who you are and fearful of what's ahead for you. Once the journey begins however, it's like you can see a tiny spark of light in the distance and, though you may stumble a few times and stop through fear, once you've started to trust, you know you can't go back to the life you came from, which was pain and suffering, so you pick yourself up and keep going.

Much of our imbalance stems from childhood and can be compounded by the way we're taught as we grow up with seemingly harmless statements from our parents, teachers or peers such as: *'You've got to put the work in at school if you're ever going to succeed in life'* or *'Be careful when you go out tonight with your friends.'* Simple and well-meaning statements such as this have an underlying message in the subconscious mind when it's something we've been used to hearing for some time. For some, these statements can go on to develop negatively compounded programmes in the mind that create fearful or adverse experiences later in life that can limit our life experience in varying degrees.

So repeatedly hearing, *'You've got to put the work in at school if you're ever going to succeed in life'*, could ultimately create negative programmes that later on as an adult push you to become a workaholic, a people-pleaser or always try to do whatever it takes to make others happy or to achieve what you think others want you to be.

When I was a little girl, I used to run up to my father, excited to share with him what I wanted to achieve, and he would always shut my enthusiasm down with: *'Don't tell me what you're going to do, tell me when you've done it.'* He was an entrepreneur and a high achiever, who excelled at everything. So, I lived life as a child feeling that I couldn't impress him. How could I ever accomplish anything that would amaze him enough, when he was the best at everything? How could I impress such greatness? It created so much fear in me consequently, that self-doubt amplified the already developed negative conditions of my upbringing, making it difficult to achieve anything. I had no idea how to impress such a giant of a man, so in the end whenever I started a new hobby or interest, I ended up giving up on it and failing. The programme I'd learned in 'giving up' stayed with me for years as an adult — through failed relationships, work commitments, security, money, health and fighting for justice. Everything I set my heart on failed.

Take a look at your own life to see if there are any areas where you feel 'out of control' and unable to make choices from your own free will; this can highlight the imbalances that may plague your life, so that you can finally do something about it. Taking that first step of recognition is also that first step into the tunnel. Remember that it only represents your transformation and that you will get through and out the other side, if you follow your angels' guidance. You can break free of the programmes that are locked in your energy field, linked with childhood in relation to family, survival, food, shelter and protection.

Deepening your inner senses not only allows you to tune into your subconscious and helps you to align with your angels, but also strengthens your relationship with yourself and lets you recognise your truth. Eventually when you discover your own uniqueness you will understand the beauty of your entire physical existence and your place in this world.

Apart from the subtle undertones of imbalances in our lives, we can also experience the obvious 'biggies' like knowing our partner is wrong for us, our job is depressing and tedious, our financial situation is at crisis point or our health is challenging us. Our angels of light are there to guide us from any dark situation (which may have multiple issues) into the light so that huge transformations can take place.

Many of us know what it's like if a colleague has had yet another argument with a family member and then comes into work and causes tension and upset around them. The office could, for example, be open plan and filled with twenty to thirty other colleagues. How many colleagues do you think working around that person will go through their day feeling dreadful themselves and become counterproductive because of that 'bad atmosphere' or tension? How many of them still will go home to their families and pass that negativity on? And so, the ripple continues. Being in alignment is not just about taking responsibility for your own energy but also stops you from passing on negativity to others, which as you can see in this example could potentially affect hundreds of people, just from one person.

Like me, you may have been suffering imbalances for many years before recognising something's wrong. It is not easy to come to terms with that — or we would all be able to 'miraculously' heal our lives with very little effort! Often, it is because the solutions we need are not obvious ones, so we simply put up with our adversities and avoid change. However, when you have a strong conviction to look beyond the obvious, you will find the solutions you need through your angels' messages. Faith always carries you through.

When we're aligned, we're able to project our goals and vision to the energy world from where our dreams can be created. Angels recognise the Creator Source within humans, which motivates them to interact with us as our preset programmes from birth are for us to learn how to love and to learn how to be creative. Therefore, unlocking your creativity will help you to develop a more intimate relationship with your angels of light.

Leave space for imagination, questions and creativity as you build relationships with your own angels and do not try to judge, grade, rate or perfect your creative work. An open mind is a powerful tool when trying to work with Divine beings. A logical, rigid way of thinking is limiting.

Another of my clients, Amara, came to me at a time when she felt lost and alone, despite being married and surrounded by family and loved ones. My angels helped me by suggesting *'Guide her to meditate and trust her visions Amanda.'* Having ignored her passion from a young age to become an artist for the sake of honouring what her family expected of her, once she started to meditate her dreams started to become a haven of creative exploration as her angels started to waken her slumbering yearning. Almost instantly, she started to paint again, replicating the images of her angels on to canvas in glorious forms. Over a period of ten years her life changed unrecognisably as her art took on a life of its own. Her angels inspired every glorious image she created and her life reflected that in ways which gave her a new sense of purpose, structure, security and adventure. Over the years, she's created over seventy works of art depicting angels in all forms, often integrating the angelic realms with our own world, inspiring others to embrace their own yearnings.

I have had many 'light bulb moments' throughout my spiritual awakening and still continue to do so today. I have learned to act upon them, even if they have scared me at first, because the results always end up being rewarding for my soul's growth. My angels would often whisper in those moments *'Pay attention to this Amanda and follow your heart despite your fears. We are always with you.'* Developing our relationship with our angels of light and trusting those 'light bulb moments' are positive as they often contain important messages from our angels, which will help us to clear our circuits and match the vibration and wholeness we seek.

Meditation – breathing exercise for alignment

Find a time when you will not be disturbed, close your eyes and breathe deeply for one minute or until you feel deeply relaxed. Allow your angel symbol to come into your mind. Visualise it as clearly as you can. If it's a scene, allow the colours, sounds, smells, tastes and perhaps the touch of things around you to heighten your inner senses until you feel you have a strong connection with that symbol. If it's a sign of some kind or even a sound, like a song you feel you resonate with to connect with your angels of light, allow it to get stronger until it feels heightened in your inner senses. Then simply ask your angels of light to guide you to see what you need to do to 'de-clutter' and what's out of balance in your life. You may not get anything at first and don't expect things to come into your mind straight away. Keep your breathing slow and calm, focus on your symbol and just allow yourself to be with this exercise and see what you 'feel'. If anything comes to you that you feel your angels are showing you, then make a note of this in your journal after this meditation and make a plan to take 'right action' to honour it.

Your light bulb moment

When I discovered 'worry baskets', still used in Native American cultures today, I created something similar inspired by my angels in the form of my own personal wooden 'imbalance box'. They explained to me how to use it. *'Each time you have a worry or concern about an imbalance in your life, write the problem on a piece of paper and place it in the box. Then, ask us to clear and shield you from that worry to help bring about resolution.'*

Make yourself an 'imbalance box' — you can use a jar, bucket, bowl or anything you can easily get your hands on

— and do the same. Each time you find that an imbalance is resolved, take that piece of paper out of your box and tear it up, discarding it purposefully while thanking your angels of light for helping you to be aligned. Remember to use your 'imbalance box' whenever you feel you need to.

Chapter summary

So, what have you learned in this chapter to enable you to talk with your angels of light? Alignment enables you to find your truth, your purpose, your people and your passion. Recognising imbalances allows opportunities for you to learn vital lessons for your soul's growth and to enable you to take right action to align yourself in order to create harmony and clearly discern what your angels of light are communicating to you, which is key.

COUNT YOUR BLESSINGS

Why do you feel blessed today?...

....

....

....

....

....

....

....

....

....

....

....

....

....

....

....

....

....

....

....

6

The Energy World

So here I sit with all I am
Your presence within me.
I dedicate my life to make
A life of harmony.

Chakras and auras

The Sanskrit word **Chakra** means 'wheel' or 'disc'. People describe these as wheels of energy throughout the body. There are many more, but there are seven main energy centres which run through the spine from the crown of the head down to the base.

We all have an aura. An **aura** is an invisible energy field that surrounds us that is constantly affected by and reacts to our thoughts, feelings, situations and people we come into contact with. Our aura is also known as our subtle energy body. Some who have highly attuned clairvoyance can see auras around people but even those who have very limited understanding of their inner senses can perceive what a person is like by tuning into that person's aura. Our angels of light connect with us through our inner senses so when we develop a balanced aura our inner senses are more attuned for greater communication.

Not only is it important to be mindful of our aura to heighten our angel communication, but the condition of our aura affects our physical body and vice versa which is governed by the Divine law of nature. Life force energy flows from the Divine, down through Chakras, also known as our psychic centres which are part of our aura. Chakras are situated a few inches in front of our body along our spine which is like a stem, the Chakras being like flowers growing from that stem. Our health and wellbeing is intricately connected to our Chakras just as much as the level of our communication with our angels of light. It is all connected.

By incorporating good practices we keep our Chakras balanced, thus creating harmony and wellbeing which enables us to better communicate with the energy world to aid a deeper communication with our angels of light. The energy world is where we receive all our insight and information from to manifest our desires. We are first and foremost energy in a physical body. Everything around us in our environment is energy likewise. Intention and thought is energy. So, if we want to achieve anything we need to put our right intention into it and, if we're in alignment, are likely to receive it if it's for our highest good.

Everything that's energy in our environment vibrates at a different frequency. Our nervous system in our body picks up energy from different things which causes different effects on us. You know what it feels like if you compare entering a busy nightclub full of people with loud music with going into the peaceful setting of a woodland scene. Our body reacts to the vibrations very differently. Angels of light are high-vibrational, which is often why we only sense them in the still quiet moments in an environment that allows us to perceive that vibration.

If we want to listen to our messages, then we must learn to be still and quiet as our angels of light are constantly trying to communicate with us, but we need to be in the right frequency and environment to interpret them. Those messages are received into our physical world so we can understand them through our seven main Chakras which align us to the energy world.

These energy wheels are where life force energy feeds us from the Divine, which keeps us healthy and alive. Each Chakra has its own function and relates to a colour. As you become more aware of colours through your visualisations, orbs or exercises which reveal colour to you, that may also give you vital clues to a deeper meaning. When talking to our angels of light for guidance, we then receive communication from them in the form of light which travels through the seven stages of manifestation. I discuss these below.

The Higher Chakras – energy world
1. The Crown — White — Inspiration — *I know* (inspiration from Source via our angels)

2. The Brow — Purple — Visualisation — *I see* (visual of inspiration)

3. The Throat — Blue — Planning and Preparation — *I hear and see* (activates a healing process)

4. The Heart — Pink or Green — Determination and Dedication — *I love* (activates the connection between the energy and physical world)

The Lower Chakras – earth world

5. The Solar Plexus — Yellow — Energy Centre — *I can* (hopes and dreams, activates personal power)

6. The Sacral — Orange — Creativity Centre — *I feel/want* (drives you into action)

7. The Base — Red — Manifestation Centre — *I have* (security/survival, grounds you to desire the basics for life i.e. food, warmth, shelter, love)

Simply put, if we ask our angels for help to create something in our lives, then we will receive an inspiration from them in our mind through our Crown. As we ponder on this, it emerges in our Brow or Third Eye Chakra as something we see. As a picture appears, it starts to stir a feeling of possibility which draws this down to our Throat Chakra. This triggers our hearing so a combination of what our angels are showing and telling us through our thoughts, prompts us to start making plans.

When we start transforming thoughts into plans it triggers the Heart Chakra and we start to build a relationship with what we're manifesting through love. This creates determination to see it through. As we draw this energy down to the Solar Plexus Chakra it starts to move into the earth world in order to become something physical. This is where our personal power resides in order to give it the momentum through our hopes and dreams. Moving into the Sacral Chakra triggers our creativity, the driving force to translate it into something physical and finally it arrives at the Base Chakra as something you have.

When we're asking for solutions to challenges in our lives then it's easy to pray and ask our angels for inspiration and guidance, but we need to be still enough to listen, see or feel the messages in order to honour and understand our guidance. Often, I hear my angels stop me in my tracks as I hear them whisper *'Pay attention to what is going on for you right now!'* When I stop and really absorb what is going on for me in that moment I realise the message, as often life becomes too chaotic for us to receive our messages through our busyness. When we really pay attention, it is then a natural progression for something to come into our life that we desire through the guidance of our angels of light through our Chakra system.

About ten years ago, I was invited to participate in the London to Brighton bike ride, which is a major cycling event in the UK for professional and novice cyclists alike. I had not ridden a bike outdoors since I was a child. I was to be part of a team of nine other cyclists as one had dropped out at the last minute. I took the challenge. Even though my friends and family thought I was bonkers for accepting this at the time, my angels of light came to me in a meditation when I checked in with them and assured me I could do it. *'Amanda, sometimes it is in doing things that we think are impossible, that the possible happens in order to teach us of greater things we can achieve.'*

As it was a fifty-four-mile race in excess of twenty-thousand competitors, I had been advised to get a decent bike. As a complete novice, I bought what most would term as a 'shopping basket' town bike, designed for pootling to the high street and back for a few groceries. I was utterly dismayed and a little embarrassed, to say the least, when I turned up to meet my team on the day and they all turned out to be personal trainers, triathletes or spin bike instructors with the very latest high-end racing bikes! I had no experience whatsoever and it was blatantly obvious to all the other cyclists who were pouring towards the start line, let alone my own team members. Still, I filled the void in the team numbers, despite them looking on at me pitifully as if to say, *'Poor girl, she hasn't got a clue what she's let herself in for.'*

When we joined the starting point, along with hundreds of other cyclists, my entire team left me behind in a haze of back tyres and dust. I was petrified because I had assumed that the London traffic would be cleared for the race, but no, I had the wave of racing bikes tearing past me *and* the notoriously busy London traffic to negotiate with. I seriously questioned my judgement — what on earth had I let myself in for? But one thing was for sure, I had received a message from my angels to inspire me to enter the race in the first place (through my Crown) and they had shown me crossing the finishing line in my meditation (through my Brow). Although feeling incredibly anxious, I had to trust they knew what was best for me. Rigidly cycling through the commotion going on all around me, I called my angels of light to help me deal with my worried thoughts.

A gentle voice of reassurance came into my mind and I instantly knew my angels were there with me. *'Just focus on staying on the bike, Amanda. We are with you,'* I heard them say, reminding me that I'd already planned and prepared for this (through my Throat) and that as long as they were with me, guiding me, I would be OK. No sooner had I heard the voice, I felt my body relax and a tingling sensation washed over my entire body. It was the strongest I'd ever felt up to that point. Then it felt as if my angels were behind me, gently pushing the bike's momentum forward and I felt an incredible surge of love from them (triggering my Heart), spurring me on with new and invigorated determination. Instantly, my legs no longer felt as tired, my anxiety faded and the lightness I felt combined with their strength seemed to propel me effortlessly through the confusion all around me. I felt my personal power centre merging with their limitless supply as if I'd just been plugged directly into the

Divine (through my Solar Plexus) and amplified to such a degree it was as if I was completely safe, cycling alone and no one noticed I was there.

Somehow, slowly navigating my way through the melee of cars, trucks and bicycles, I surprised myself by managing to find my way through the urban chaos and into the rural countryside. Once there I started to breathe deeply. I was starting to relax into the flow, feeling remarkably at ease the more distance I covered.

My angels showed me that I was the tortoise in the story of 'The Hare and the Tortoise' and that the hundreds of bikes continually speeding past me represented the hare. A vision appeared in my mind, full of vivid and vibrant colours and the comforting feeling of my childhood storybook animation. Then my angels said: *'Remember this story, Amanda? This will be a life lesson for the future in understanding how effectively you can move through life with ease, despite the challenges.'*

So, with a burst of energy driving me into action (through my Sacral) and feeling encouraged by the reassurance that my angels of light were showing me a valuable life lesson, I kept peddling. There were regular stop points along the route marked out and at each refreshment point I passed, there were multitudes of cyclists relaxing and recouping after each section they'd blasted through, but my angels told me just to keep going at my own pace. Whenever a moment of doubt or exhaustion started to kick in, their words of, *'Just keep going Amanda'*, cut through any self-sabotaging moments.

I continued to peddle on past stop points, past those who had given up or had difficulties with injuries or bike malfunctions. I continued past major incidents with my eyes closed, and up hills, regardless of how my legs felt when they were on fire from the intense pain. Dark thoughts tried to continually creep into my head to convince me to give up when my body was in immense pain. The very physical act of keeping going through that long-distance endurance challenge was certainly more mental than physical. During the tough moments, my angels spoke to me reassuringly that I would not only finish, but the experience would always remain with me to never give up when faced with challenges of endurance in the future. I trusted their guidance implicitly and pushed through, despite the pain. When I freewheeled down hills and felt the reward of the respite, my angels encouraged me to see that was a lesson too.

'Enjoy the moments Amanda, as they will rejuvenate you between the tough times.'

Eventually, I got to the finish line, much to my own and everyone else's amazement (arriving at the end result at the Base).

When our team finally met back at the van to go home and we got our finishing times, it came to light that I had actually come third in our group! The experience has served me well in life as my angels taught me to always go at my own pace, on my own terms, regardless of what's going on around me.

We can't go through life avoiding dark places and in actual fact some of the most illuminating experiences come to us in or after the darkest of moments You are more resilient than you perhaps believe.

You need never be afraid to step into the darkness in order to notice the light that shines brightly from your angels of light through you — just as I dug deep into the dark corners of my mind to communicate with my angels of light, who helped me to tap into the emotional resilience that enabled me to power on through the London to Brighton bike ride!

Affirmations for the Chakras

Crown — *I am whole and complete and at one with the Divine*

Brow — *I trust and am open to Divine inspiration, the all-seeing, all-knowing*

Throat — *My thoughts are positive and I express myself with authenticity*

Heart — *I am open, unconditionally loving and connected to all that is*

Solar Plexus — *I am powerful and purposeful in all that I do that serves the greater good*

Sacral — *I express myself creatively, honouring beauty and passion in my life for good health*

Base — *I am safe, secure and grounded, grateful for my existence here on earth*

Client example of using the Chakras to talk with angels of light

Angels can guide you to people in the most diverse situations. I was on holiday in Africa and briefly got to know someone in my hotel — a young British woman who was living in Australia. During our conversation, it was apparent that my angels of light had guided me to her. We exchanged numbers. A few weeks later, she contacted me to ask me to help her. Claire loved her life and her job as a professional make-up artist, meeting interesting clients, but she was concerned about money, security and of course whether she would eventually receive her full citizenship. Her life was filled with highs and lows and she yearned for balance.

Claire was very open to new ideas as she had already experienced synchronicity in many ways but often felt disconnected and unsure sometimes of her signs. She believed her angels were trying to communicate with her often but didn't quite understand what those messages meant at times. I recommended using flower remedies for her emotions (as emotions link directly to the Chakras) and affirmations to clear the blocks in her energy system.

Within a short space of time, Claire started to attract more clients and even embarked on new projects which honoured her spiritual nature to help women going through cancer treatment. She started to feel the richness from giving her time freely.

Claire found that the more she worked to keep her Chakras in balance through positive and healthy practices, the more her desires unfolded. Finding her communication with her angels unfolding and moving away from habits that had blocked her in the past opened her up to a whole new world of supportive relationships and opportunities, helping her expand her business, meeting the love of her life, who she moved in with, and finally allowing her the understanding that she has the power to communicate with her angels of light whenever she wants to enhance her life and find solutions. Claire finally got her citizenship and all the things she wanted to manifest and is now an inspiration to others across the world. She regularly shares her wisdom to her vast network which comes to her through her angels of light.

Meditation to clear and cleanse the Solar Plexus Chakra

This meditation allows you to balance between the intuition and intellect to develop your relationship with your self-esteem, personal power and your relationship with your environment and your place in this world. This enables you to be more accepting of the workings of the energy world and the way your angels of light communicate with you. Working with this Chakra balances what becomes possible through the harmony of the upper four and lower three Chakras.

First, find a warm and comfortable place to sit or lie down where you won't be disturbed. Light a candle if you can and, if you like to use crystals, choose any or a combination of the following:

Pyrite

Citrine

Orange Calcite

Tiger's Eye

Yellow Agate

Shungite

You can use any yellow stones so choose the ones that speak to you. Pyrite, for instance, holds the energy of a ray of golden sun.

If you are lying down, place the crystals on your lower abdomen above your belly button. If you are sitting, make sure you sit upright in a comfortable position either cross-legged if you can on the floor or, if you're sitting in a chair, place your feet flat on the ground (uncrossed) and have your hands gently cupped facing upward in your lap with the crystals (if you so choose) placed in your hands. You can record this meditation and play it back to yourself, so you can use it any time you feel you need an energy boost, need some balance in your life and to heighten your inner senses.

Close your eyes and focus on breathing in and out for the count of four for approximately one minute, or for as long as you feel necessary, until you start to feel your physical body relax. Starting with the top of your head, breathe into it. Let go of any tension and feel the top of your head loosen and release. Move down to your face, back of the head and ears. Sense anywhere you're holding on to stress and breathe into it, letting it go. Move your focus now down to your throat and neck and check that the muscles are not taut. Breathe into any areas that feel rigid until you feel the muscles unwind.

Now take your focus down to your shoulders, arms, hands, chest and upper back. Breathe and let go of any tension. When you're ready, move on down to your stomach and the middle of your back. Focus this time on bringing the breath down into your belly on every in breath and, as you breathe out, let it rise all the way up to your crown to release.

When you feel ready, take your attention down to your lower abdomen and lower back. Keep breathing deeply and letting go. Then, move your focus to your pelvis, hips, buttocks, legs and feet. If there is uncertainty, breathe into that but don't judge it, just note where that uncertainty lies in your body and let it go.

Finally, when you feel your body is calm and deeply relaxed, imagine you have a channel of bright yellow light pouring on to the Crown Chakra on top of your head. This light is beaming down from Source and, as you feel the magnitude of its warmth seeping through you gradually, imagine the light is healing and restoring your mind, body and, soul completely as it pours down through each one of your Chakras: your Brow, your Throat, your Heart and let it anchor into your Solar Plexus.

Allow the light to flow on down through your Sacral and your Base. Finally let the light travel slowly down your legs to your toes. Imagine the light beaming out of you into the ground and down to the earth's core. Once it hits the centre of the earth, know that you are fully anchored to Source. Acknowledge the light charging through your entire being, like an internal shower of light, which is cleansing, purifying and rejuvenating your every cell.

Sit for a while as each Chakra absorbs the healing light from Source. Allow your inner senses to speak to you, letting you know how you feel as the radiant light glows throughout your entire body.

Sit with this thought for a while. Enjoy feeling lighter and breathe lightly so as not to interrupt this moment. You are restoring your energy body to its natural balance and harmony. Relax and enjoy this for as long as it feels right and good for you.

When you are ready to return, picture the yellow light travelling back up towards you from the earth's core, through your legs, up through your hips and pelvis to your Solar Plexus and imagine a beautiful ball of yellow light is forming now, rotating and shining brighter to fill your entire centre, from your own core. Know that when you come out of the meditation, this purifying light will continue to work with you for as long as you need to feel energised. Observe a shaft of light moving up through the rest of your body and out through your Crown Chakra, while the ball of light continues to rotate soothingly in your core.

Slowly open your eyes and come back into the room knowing that you will carry that ball of perfect yellow light around with you through which your angels of light can communicate with you more clearly now that your personal power has returned and your Chakras have been cleansed, rejuvenated and aligned for your highest good. It will continue to help you find alignment in your outer and inner world, continuing to enhance your angel communication. You should now feel calm, happier, lighter and more focused at the end of this practice.

Your light bulb moment

I've loved working with and teaching clients to use imagery-based card decks for many years. It's a powerful way to help clients when they overthink life and to find those light bulb moments induced visually from our angels of light. This is a quick and easy way to start to introduce yourself to reading cards.

Firstly, if you don't have your own deck of cards, explore what you feel drawn to. There is a huge array to choose from, so find what resonates and speaks to you first. As with all tools and talismans, keeping them in a safe and respectful place will amplify their energy each time you work with them.

Find a quiet space and focus on something that concerns you or a question you wish your angels to answer for you. I use three cards for simplicity as this is all you really need until you wish to explore further.

Take a few deep breaths and relax and share with your angels of light your concern or question. Shuffle the cards with your eyes closed and choose three randomly from the pack and, with your eyes open, place them down in order, face up so that you can see each card you've chosen.

Spend a moment allowing the images of the cards to speak to you. Reflect on each card in the order that you drew them as these cards are a channel from your angels of light to trigger memories, words, stories or perhaps associations in relation to what your concern is.

- **The first card** — should reflect your current situation or concern.
- **The second card** — should reflect the reason why this situation has occurred or the lesson that you need to see.
- **The third card** — is the action your angels of light are getting you to take to overcome or solve your situation.

This is an incredibly insightful way that your angels of light can communicate with you. Record your concern or question in your journal and what you've discovered in your three-card spread. This takes practice, trust and patience, so if you don't get something that stands out to you immediately, practise and play at this. The more relaxed you are, the more you'll see.

Chapter summary

So, what have you learned in this chapter to enable you to talk with your angels of light? Your angels of light communicate with you through your inner senses which are linked to your energy field. Your seven main Chakras need to be in balance to allow that smooth flow of communication from your angels of light to come through and to promote good health and wellbeing. Becoming respectful of your Chakras and their crucial role allows you to manifest your desires, heightening your inner senses for a deeper communication with your angels of light.

COUNT YOUR BLESSINGS

Why do you feel blessed today?...

....

....

....

....

....

....

....

....

....

....

....

....

....

....

....

....

....

7

Healing

You're morning sun and painted rose
A whisper through the trees.
Your healing is in everything
Like nectar from the bees.

When I first discovered my yearning to heal, it was to let
go of what no longer served me and opened me to a whole
new incredible world of enlightenment and possibility. As
the burdens of my past released and my Mind, Body, Spirit
healed, my life started to reflect what I never thought could
be possible as light started to burst into every corner of my
world.

When I started to work with clients, I discovered that
most visiting me had some kind of health issue, even though
it wasn't the primary concern for wanting to see me. Our
angels of light are natural healers and I have always called
upon them to heal myself, loved ones, clients and situations.
Their light is a rich and infinite source of positive energy

and unconditional love capable of transmuting darkness in all guises to a state of balance and harmony. Calling upon our angels of light can heal anything that is out of balance in our life.

Self-improvement

My father, a very pragmatic man, told me a story that changed his rejection of spirituality. When he was a young man, he was riding his motorbike home as dusk settled in one evening; the light was poor and he was tired after yet another long day at work. Dad misjudged a bend at speed and went hurtling towards a six-foot-high wall! Suddenly, an elderly lady appeared directly in his path. He tried to brake but his bike went from underneath him and started sliding towards her with him rolling alongside it.

Before impact the lady just seemed to disappear. When Dad was over the initial shock of everything that happened, he got himself up and assessed the situation searching for the lady. To his astonishment, he heard her on the other side of the wall. He carefully nursed his own injuries and hauled himself over the wall, while wondering how she had managed to scale it. He expected to see her dreadfully wounded, but she was calm when he found her — sitting, quite comfortably, in a bed of leaves that had cushioned her fall.

Dad asked the lady how on earth she'd got over such a tall wall so quickly. She described watching him about to crash into her and thinking her life was over, and then somehow being lifted up *'by an angel'* and thrown to safety, landing miraculously where he'd found her. There was not a single scratch on her! In fact, *she* ended up comforting my father until an ambulance arrived.

Angels are not just there as rescuers but are sent to assist us with honouring our blueprint, which sets out our best health and wellbeing, relationships and life's purpose. I believe my father was being shown a vital lesson from angels that day to teach him about being less reckless. It was perhaps a call to action for him to slow down (not just in that moment on his bike, but in his life too). That message could well have been telling him that moving through life at breakneck speed would not be best for his overall health and wellbeing. When we move away from the essence of who we are, angels of light are there to assist us to get back to who we are in order to honour our best selves and heal.

Healing ourselves is of paramount importance in order for us to heal our world and the people around us. Looking after our body is most important but we are all unique, so by being more grounded or centred, naturally we intuitively become more aware of what nutrition works for us.

It's incredible to think that we haven't evolved that much in the last few thousand years compared to how our diets have radically changed, and much of our food is crippled with substances that our immune systems are constantly too overworked to deal with. Nourishing food is key and the simpler the better. I'm not saying that we should all radicalise

115

our diets to living off water and lettuce leaves but becoming more mindful of what we ingest will help us to take back our power and allow our bodies to become more stabilised — after all, this is the only vehicle we get in this lifetime.

Restoration

When I was thirty-six, quite suddenly I ended up seriously ill in hospital and had my own near-death experience. Many people who know me well say that when I was discharged, I was no longer the same person who had gone into that hospital. I'd arrived in the accident and emergency department as a victim, fearful of my whole life and seemingly powerless, but what I experienced changed my whole attitude to life in an instant.

I knew it was serious as I could hear through the commotion of instructions being shouted by the doctors and nurses running around and several voices telling me what they were doing to me, someone shout that they had better get my husband in quickly. Despite the excruciating pain, I could feel myself slipping in and out of consciousness and at one point I realised that I was actually going to die. A sense of peace washed over me which was surprising as, up to that point, my experience had been days of debilitating discomfort.

My eyes were closed as I couldn't take the light but as soon as I felt myself slipping away, the voices in the accident and emergency room faded into the background and an angel appeared in front of my eyes with an incredible light that filled the mental screen of my mind and spoke to me.

'Amanda, you are not ready to go yet, but it's your choice. You have much more to give than you realise. Your children need you, you have insight to share and work to be done to help others but you have to decide if you want to change in order to honour your truth.'

It was like a dawn of realisation as I was shown my children and all that I'd gone through in what seemed like hours, but must actually have been seconds. Then the angel took my arms which were both wired to drips and carefully placed my hands palms down on my stomach.

'You can heal yourself Amanda. Trust,' the angel said, and then slowly faded away.

From that moment even though I couldn't see that angel, I felt the presence of angels all around my bed as if they were watching over me in a vigil. I felt swaddled in what seemed like a nest of angel wings. I was in and out of consciousness for several days but, throughout, I felt them with me.

In my early days exploring healing, my angels would appear as white orbs on different parts of my client's body to alert me to what was wrong with them, with their health. This was particularly helpful when the client didn't consciously recognise they had an issue until I asked them about it and then they would make a connection perhaps to an old injury or an imbalance in their body which would have some significance. Over the years, I have learned that different coloured orbs mean different things to me, and these colours will mean different things to different people.

It is important to see what comes to you intuitively when you recognise colours in some way, especially with orbs or in visualisations and dreams, so that you can build a personal language with your angels of light.

Nutrition

Our angels communicate with us through our inner senses remember and our Solar Plexus is where our clairsentience resides, our intuitive faculty or gut instinct. It's where we feel what our angels are communicating to us and it can be far more subtle than the other two senses. I learned many years ago through great teachers that it's the most important. It often backs up what we are seeing and hearing, but it links with our instincts to survive in this world and therefore when we have a 'clear' personal power centre, as opposed to a slow and clogged one, we have a far stronger communication with our angels of light. Many light workers (which I go into more detail about in Chapter 8), instinctively eat mindfully because their angels communicate this to them through the very sense they wish them to enhance. Our imbalances, when addressed, reveal a deepening connection with our angels of light to find our strengths, our personal power and purpose.

I discovered through one insightful teacher that asking my angels of light to bless our food has an amazing effect on its absorption. I've asked them to bless the food I'm making for my family since. Try saying something positive to each meal before you eat it for the next seven days and see if you notice the difference in your energy. Look at what you're about to eat and say something like: *'Angels of light, thank you for this wonderful food. Please bless this so our bodies use all the nutrients for our highest good, with ease.'* Focusing on your food and loving every mouthful has a massively beneficial effect on your whole digestive process.

Detoxing is a great way of allowing the body to ease up, let go and rest. Some choose to go on retreats to allow for the 'whole experience' and some choose to do it for a whole day, once a month. Whatever you choose to do and in whatever way best serves you, giving your body some time out from all that processing of food gives it time to heal.

The healing power of nature

Many years ago I was introduced to the concept of Ho'oponopono, an ancient forgiveness and reconciliation practice from Hawaiian tradition. The ritual is said to cleanse 'errors of thought' which are the origin of problems and sickness in the physical world to put them right and create order.

My life was in crisis and my angels suggested I speak to a friend. *'Your friend Gareth will provide you with a solution Amanda.'* I had no idea what that could be but invited him to stay all the same and during his visit with me he suggested we go for a walk and try some healing. I didn't hesitate. We were walking in the woods, along one of the regular routes that I took with my dog, when Gareth suggested, '*Let's try to identify and alleviate your fears, Amanda.*'

We both knew I was not able to see my own negative programme that was blocking me, so he talked me through the process. When I focused and looked at what the source of the problem originated from it was a light bulb moment as the answer just came to me as clear as anything.

'*It's success! That's what it is – fear of success. Every time I've created something, whether it be a business, a relationship, a home, or a project of any kind, somehow, I lose it or it's destroyed. I can see it now,*' I replied triumphantly.

This all stemmed back to my childhood as my father's whole motivation was about succeeding. But in the end, he lost everything, including me, his wealth, all he worked for and created and, finally, he lost his own life. I could see it so clearly as I'd been following his patterns. Every relationship I had was doomed to fail and each time I tried to build a business or home I ended up losing them.

When a powerful spotlight is shone on the destructive patterns of our mind it can be incredibly empowering. The insight gained over the course of my years of struggle, was like waking to see a beautiful panoramic view on a bright summer's day, after having been partially sighted for years.

Once I'd identified with that fear, I spoke out loud the words to the part of me that needed to hear, '*I'm sorry. Please forgive me. I love you. Thank you.*' I knew then that I would fully accept and love that part of me that needed to heal.

I was amazed by the lightness I felt as we continued with our walk through the woods. It was as if all the negativity was washing down through me into the earth, cleansing my entire being. It felt as if nature was holding me, nurturing and cleansing me from the inside out. It felt like a warm and tender hug from the inside. As I continued to walk, I noticed a lightness and how I was breathing fully into my lungs for the first time in a long, long while.

That healing had a profound effect on me. I was finally able to physically heal and everything I created from then on was built on firm foundations, supported by those who served my highest good and still continues to grow today. Try this for yourself. It's an incredible form of healing.

There are strong links between nature and our angels too as they both contain the blueprint for perfection and unconditional love. Nature speaks to our higher self, imitating the love of our angels, such as the season of spring which signifies hope, rebirth, new life and lighter days, etc. When we observe or immerse ourselves in nature we have a propensity to be filled with awe and wonder. I believe our angels are communicating something Divine to us to show us we already have what we believe is heaven, on earth.

I've had a special relationship with nature since I was three years old and spent countless hours as a child in my garden at home, where I felt held and healed by nature. It was where I felt closest to my angels, received their healing light in a dark world of despair and often they would reassure me with *'Amanda, this is your safe place where you will always feel us with you. Nature reflects the unconditional love we are teaching you in all ways.'* Throughout my adult life my relationship has deepened with nature which has constantly nurtured, cleansed and energised my soul.

Spending time in nature, immersing yourself in nature, allows your body to not only ground itself, but to heal and open to the higher blueprint of nature to enhance your inner senses. Mindfully walking in nature connects the blueprint of nature with ourselves thus elevating our awareness.

Many cultures have celebrated nature from the earliest records of humanity, especially during the spring equinox (or autumn equinox in the southern hemisphere) to bring new light into our lives and therefore enhance creating new situations. Spring is a season of hope and new beginnings, of rebirth and colour re-emerging. The equinox is a time when the sun crosses the equator, moving northward which provides the earth's hemispheres with equal amounts of sunlight. This creates days and nights of approximate equal length around the world.

Equinoxes were important in ancient cultures and human civilisations throughout history incorporated these significant dates into their cultural and religious practices. Today, a whole host of evidence of these practices have been created through the buildings and structures our ancestors left behind.

People travel to places all over the world for the equinox to celebrate new beginnings, rejuvenation and rebirth. Many ancient civilisations created structures to experience the sunlight's role in announcing the new season and archaeologists believe that, during ancient times, kings wanted to connect the earth with the sky so built temples to integrate both all over the world. Perhaps you've visited or wish to visit one yourself.

Here are some to consider:

- **Chichen Itza** was one of the largest built ancient Mayan cities and thrived from around AD 600. Today it's one of the most visited architectural sites in Mexico. People travel there especially on the equinoxes, to witness the sun casting shadows on the steps of the Temple of Kukulkan, which gives the illusion that a serpent is slithering down the pyramid's steps. The symbol of a serpent in Mayan culture, much like a snake, was believed to represent the shedding of the skin for rebirth.

- **Angkor Wat**, a temple complex built in the first half of the twelfth century, is the largest religious monument in the world and is not only one of Cambodia's largest tourist attractions but appears on their national flag. The sun rises exactly on the peak of the main Angkor Temple twice a year at the equinoxes which makes us wonder how these ancient civilisations could master such a task to time what governs the sky with what we create here on earth.

- **Basilica di San Petronio** is the main church of Bologna, Italy, and one of the largest churches in the world.

Building began in 1390, however, it's still unfinished today. An original sundial was built in the church by Dante but was damaged and later restructured and improved by Cassini, an Italian astronomer, to study the movement of the sun throughout the year. By the eleventh century, the sundial was used to accurately determine the date of the spring equinox using the longest indoor meridian line in the world.

- **Stonehenge** in Wiltshire, England, is the most famous prehistoric monument and is still a destination for those looking to celebrate the equinoxes. Stonehenge is made up of a ring of standing stones and set within a group of Neolithic and Bronze Age monuments, as well as several hundred burial mounds. Now managed by English Heritage, the site opens for visitors at dawn for each equinox and solstice event, so that druids, pagans and other earth worshipers can watch the sun rise on the ancient stones.

I was guided to visit the Great Sphinx in Egypt for the spring equinox which was an incredibly memorable event. It will always remain in my heart as the whole trip was an enlightened lesson on spiritual growth which my angels guided me through, step by step, temple by temple, until I reached the Pyramids of Giza, where the Sphinx is situated.

Having gone with a group of forty, gathered for the spring equinox, we stood in quiet contemplation and one minute I was there, the next I was gone. I felt I'd fallen down an elevator shaft deep into the earth. It was the Emerald City as I called it, which I'd often seen in recurring dreams as a child. Just like in my dreams, I was there again, walking down a path with other people, which ran alongside a stream in a tranquil and beautiful place. There were flowers and trees of all kinds and birds of many varieties and vast expanses of grass. The place was rich and abundant with colour and life. It was a place of belonging and safety, a place where harmony was the fabric of life.

I hadn't thought of that dream once as an adult, but standing between the paws of the Sphinx I felt my angels close, sharing with me the significance of how this dream would shape my life. *'This is a significant time for you Amanda. Your life will finally reveal your authentic self to find that peace and fulfilment that you deserve.'* And they were right.

The Sphinx faces the sun as it rises in the east and it is said that this cycle continues for 2160 years during the same zodiac sign. Then on the day of a spring equinox, at sunrise, the sign is replaced by the next zodiac sign, dawning a new age! This cycle continues through all twelve astrological signs for a total of 26,000 years. This spectacular statue I later found out has links also with the stone circle in Avebury, Wiltshire, which I was often drawn to but never knew why until I made the link.

My angels would often encourage me to go to Avebury to visit the famous stone circle. This is just part of a set of ceremonial sites spread out around the area, built between 2850 BC and 2200 BC, but the stone circle itself, fascinated me most.

My angels asked me to walk into the Tourist Information Office there one day, where they led me to a folder of newspaper cuttings. Leafing through I found an article about a researcher who had found a remarkable link with one of the stones at Avebury and the Sphinx in Egypt. The researcher had taken a photo of one of the main stones and recreated it as a mirror-image (like a butterfly). This image looked incredibly like the Sphinx itself, leading him to believe that originally the stone in Avebury had resembled the mighty image in Egypt but at some point had been cut in half. On further investigation, he found that the placement of the stone was not only linked to the Orion belt pattern, as was the Sphinx, but looking at latitude lines, they also matched and both faced the east to welcome the morning sun.

Over the years, I've travelled to many sacred sites to honour the spring equinox, just like when I had the chance to stand between the paws of the mighty Sphinx itself. With the body of a lion and the head of a pharaoh, it has the most enigmatic gaze as if it holds many secrets.

If you can't travel you can still make the most of nature around you. In your home, you can create an oasis of indoor plants that will thrive but make sure you choose what will grow in your particular environment. Sitting with plants or even holding your hands over them for a few minutes will allow you to experience the restorative sensations you will receive. Allowing your plants to absorb any toxins and cleanse your energy field for just a few minutes every day will make a difference.

Visiting your local park, natural space or heritage sites, for instance, gives you a chance to walk in nature allowing Mother Earth to relax, rejuvenate and energise you. Make it part of your daily or weekly routine and walk as often as you can. The more natural your surroundings, the better.

Even having a small place in your garden, like a bench where you like to sit, a summer house, conservatory or even a garden shed, enables you to invite nature to hold you in that moment. The most important thing to remember is that wherever *you* are drawn to for your own natural sanctuary is what counts.

Woodland and forests are my favourite and where I prefer to go to walk my dog as often as possible. The trees with all their wisdom and magnificence remind us of our angels' presence and where I communicate with them the most. Angels love us to be in nature as it's the easiest medium to connect with us through.

I love the Japanese concept of Shinrin-Yoku or 'forest bathing'. Developed during the 1980s, it has become a foundation of preventive healthcare and healing in Japanese medicine. Research now shows that the health benefits of spending time under the canopy of a living forest has phenomenal benefits. By simply walking in nature in a relaxed way there are calming, rejuvenating and restorative benefits to be achieved as we automatically go into the alpha state which boosts our immune system, therefore restoring and rejuvenating our entire bodies. The benefits are too numerous to mention but include reducing stress and blood pressure, and improving our focus, energy levels, sleep and mood. It deepens our connection to our inner senses, our relationships with others and our flow of life. Overall, it increases our sense of happiness.

When you make the decision to embrace your spiritual awakening, it allows you to 'draw the curtains open' to receive the golden sunlight and allow the light from your angels to pour in. This empowers you to start embracing an authentic life with an open heart, free from debilitating fear, knowing you're always protected by your angels. This, in turn, allows you to find your own personal power and the infinite power from Source, to continually energise and nurture you.

One of my clients, Alison, came to me because she was unhappy in her work and had a complicated relationship with herself, others and money, as a result of insecurities from her childhood. She had a particularly low sense of self-worth because her twin sister had found love and another of her siblings was incredibly academic and successful. Alison felt she had nothing to offer this world in comparison.

During our first session together, I guided Alison through the healing meditation until she was fully relaxed. Afterwards, she explained that on the mental screen of her mind, she saw an image of a beach scene appear and she started to feel an overwhelming sense through her Solar Plexus that she wanted to live by the coast in Cornwall. She found this surprising as she'd never even visited that part of the country. I advised her to watch out for the signs as it was most certainly a message from her angels of light and that, when the signs came, she should take the right action. A couple of weeks after that session, she was invited to stay with a friend who lived in Cornwall! Alison contacted me immediately, feeling incredibly excited that her angels had been so clear to her.

During Alison's visit, her friend took her to a local beach which she instantly recognised as the one she'd described in our session — the landscape was identical. It was, for Alison, a monumental 'light bulb moment' as she realised she had found the place where she knew she would live and find happiness. During our next few sessions, we continued to work with the healing meditation and I encouraged Alison to spend time in nature and to become mindful of her nutrition. She even started yoga to help her become more 'flexible' as her inevitable life change started to reveal itself. As Alison started to heal, she began to 'close the curtains' on her negative habits, relationships and beliefs that were preventing her from finding her truth and her focus started unfolding on 'opening the curtains', to unlock her power, purpose and full potential.

Alison became very motivated by the signs her angels of light were showing her and, as each sign appeared, she honoured the changes she needed to make in her life in order to make this important transition both physically and spiritually. When she faced tough times, she asked her angels of light to help her see she was on the right path to honour her truth, which they did, and six months later she attracted a job opportunity practically opposite the beach where it had all begun for her — it was perfect! The old Alison would not have had the confidence to apply, but the new Alison was channelling the light of her angels, dazzled in her interview and was offered the job a few days later! She was astounded when she got the happy news.

With only three weeks before she was due to start the job and her new life, Alison hit a new obstacle that created a sudden 'fault' in her personal energy circuit; she didn't know how she would possibly afford to rent a new home in Cornwall with her limited funds! By then she was getting more self-assurance that her angels were taking care of all the details as she was constantly finding feathers, which were her sign to trust them. I encouraged her to talk with her angels before she went to sleep one night in order to ask for their help with this. Within a few days, she was communicating with someone online who happened to be looking for a house-sitter for several months for his home in the area she was moving to, free of charge, while he went on a sailing trip. It seemed too good to be true but Alison by then knew that her angels of light had guided her to him.

Alison listened to her angels and took a leap of faith by accepting the offer from this complete stranger who she knew nothing about. At one time she would have never even dared consider such a risk, but on this occasion, she trusted her deepening relationship with her angel messengers. She moved into the house shortly before she started her new job, which gave her enough time to get her bearings in the local area and meet the owner of the house properly before he left to go travelling.

Alison not only moved to her dream location, but she found a job she enjoyed and a solution to her money-related issues which honoured her calling. She joined clubs and activities such as sailing and rafting, which helped her to get fit and healthy too, which supported and nurtured her newly aligned and healed self. Her confidence grew as she made a whole tribe of new friends, and she says she has to '*pinch herself every day*' to remind herself that she's actually living her dream.

Alison paid close attention to her 'light bulb moment', trusted her developing inner senses and angel guidance, and honoured the steps she needed to take in order to reach her ultimate goal. Her new-found life is full of adventure and authentic relationships, which have enriched her soul day by day. She is an inspiration to others and a reminder to you to pay attention to your light bulb moments and honour the process this book presents to you.

Meditation – healing in nature

This is a lovely exercise for you to enjoy in a tranquil place in nature, preferably with trees. Be open to your experience and aware as you allow your senses to blossom. Again, you can record this slowly, allowing for pauses, and play it back to yourself whenever you feel inspired to.

Travel to your chosen location. Find a place to start that you feel will allow you to be mindful of your surroundings. You can sit or stand – whatever makes you feel most comfortable. Close your eyes and allow yourself to open up to the sounds around you. Let the sounds come to you naturally. Touch your ears and feel the wrinkles and folds of your ears and lobes. Become aware of the outside of your ears and the inner ears. Relax and let the sounds wash over you. Let your hearing be soft, expansive and open. Don't judge the sounds, just let them filter into your awareness as they will. You may hear the wind in the trees, birdsong, the rustling of animals in the undergrowth. You may even hear people talking nearby, cars in the distance or a plane in the sky. Whatever you hear, just welcome everything in.

Now allow yourself to open to sight. Gently touch your closed eyes and feel your eyelids, your eyelashes and the surface of your eyes. Feel all around your eyes from the centre, into the eye sockets, up to the eyebrows that protect your eyes. Then open your eyes gently and let your gaze remain soft. Allow yourself to see your environment through your peripheral vision. As if becoming part of nature, quietly remain open to the scene around you. Allow all the colours to come to you, let the light, shadow and different textures take form but don't focus on any one thing. Just let it all gently seep into your eyes.

Go with your own gentle rhythm and, when you feel ready to, start to take a calm stroll to wherever your inner senses guide you. Don't think it. Feel it and allow yourself to be open to wander wherever your senses want to take you.

Begin to take in the fragrance that's around you. Become aware of the scent in the air but don't try to identify scents, nor judge them as 'nice, or 'bad'. Just allow your nose to guide you. Let your nose lead you through the different smells, guiding you to be closer to objects perhaps to receive the fragrance more fully. Just allow the fragrance to wash into you.

Now be open to receiving inner wisdom. Allow your awareness to focus your eyes on specific objects in your environment. Seek out colour, texture, shapes and form or anything that stands out or is interesting to you. Choose different objects to focus on and move closer to them one at a time, to really study them. Touch and feel the textures. Are they warm or cold, rough or smooth, large or small? Can you hold the object in your hand like a leaf perhaps? Perhaps rub the leaf between the palms of your hand and then smell its fragrance. Try to go deeper by studying your object in its minutest detail. Then, if it's a leaf, toss it into the air playfully and watch it get caught by the breeze and land in front of you.

Be open to receive taste. If you find something in the environment that you can experiment with, like berries, a blade of green grass, a vegetable, etc. (but be mindful that what you choose is edible), then close your eyes and allow

133

your taste buds to absorb the different flavours with that
item sat on your tongue. Do this for as long as you feel
guided to.

After twenty minutes or so of absorbing nature and
becoming mindful of your environment, notice what has
happened to you, and how these experiences have enhanced
your sense of sound, sight, smell, touch, taste and time.
Above all, how do you feel?

Your light bulb moment

Take an opportunity to see what perhaps needs healing in your life. Using the concept of Ho'oponopono, find a time when you won't be disturbed and, with your journal next to you to make notes after, close your eyes and think of anything you feel may be out of balance, where pain occurs or there is an obvious health concern. It may be an injury, condition, weight issue or attitude towards something that is causing you upset.

Once you've chosen that issue, close your eyes and, after taking some deep breaths, ask your angels of light to guide you to any underlying reason why this matter exists. It may not come to you straight away but ask that it will come to you when the time is right.

When you're ready to release and heal that part of you, regardless of whether you know or understand the underlying reason for it, speak out loud the words to the part of you that needs to hear, *'I'm sorry. Please forgive me. I love you. Thank you.'*

Know then that you will fully accept and love that part of you that needs to heal. Sit with that until you feel that healing has occurred.

When you open your eyes, record your thoughts in your journal and add to them if you have any messages from your angels after this exercise which shed some light on your situation. Be mindful over time of any changes you may go through and record those too.

You can use this exercise as often as you need to heal ALL situations whenever they present themselves, asking your angels to always help you see the lesson you need to know first. Healing is not just about overcoming imbalance as it always provides us with profound lessons that we will grow from too.

Chapter summary

So, what have you learned in this chapter to enable you to talk with your angels of light? Your angels of light are there to help you heal all areas of your life, replacing light where darkness once resided. Healing improves your life in all ways creating the balance and harmony you seek. Improving your environment is key to communicating with your angels, so becoming mindful of what you ingest through the situations in your life and what food you eat should reflect that. Spending time with nature and visiting sacred sites feeds your soul reminding you of your Divine self.

COUNT YOUR BLESSINGS

Why do you feel blessed today? . . .

....

....

....

....

....

....

....

....

....

....

....

....

....

....

....

....

....

....

....

....

8

Light Work

So here I sit with all I am
Your presence within me.
I dedicate my life to make
A life of harmony.

What is light work?

There is something innately built into the human psyche that drives us to become our best selves. This is work and I don't mean like a 9-to-5 kind of work. I mean light work: dedication and commitment in the face of life's challenges head-on. Light work brings riches and rewards beyond our comprehension. Light work is embracing our ultimate truth as human beings, although it is not as simple as not telling lies! It is a lifelong commitment to becoming aligned, overcoming challenges, heartache and honouring one's truth. We all have a truth and purpose here to play out while we reside on this earth whether it be to make a difference with the planet itself, the animal or human kingdoms.

Famous examples of light workers
throughout history

Here are some incredibly influential inspirers we've known through history and each one of them shares a common thread — they honoured their truth despite opposition.

The Greek philosopher Socrates (469 – 399 BC) was arrested for his philosophical teachings and was prepared to accept death rather than change his opinions and beliefs.

Jesus (AD 0 – 33) never wavered from the truth of the message he shared to the people despite the consequences. Even when he had the opportunity to escape or change his message he didn't. Eventually he felt the right thing to do was to suffer humiliation and pain to enable him to leave his legacy of spiritual truth.

Boudicca (AD 30 – 61), the Celtic queen of the Iceni tribe, in what is modern-day East Anglia, led a British revolt against Roman occupation.

Galileo (1564 – 1642) challenged the orthodoxy of the church through his own scientific discoveries. He committed himself to truth and science despite personal threats to his wellbeing.

Mother Teresa (1910 – 97), who was born in Albania, left for India with hardly any money and devoted her life to helping the poor of Calcutta to overcome poverty and disease. She went on to expand her mission to support the poor and disadvantaged across the world.

Nelson Mandela (1918 – 2013) had the courage to fight against apartheid. For his political activities, he was sentenced to life in prison, but was later released to lead a free, desegregated South Africa.

The 14th Dalai Lama (1935 –), the spiritual and political leader of the Tibetan people, led non-violent resistance to Chinese rule in Tibet.

Malala Yousafzai (1997 –), a Pakistani schoolgirl who defied threats to campaign for the right to education. She survived being shot in the head by the Taliban and has become a worldwide advocate for human rights, women's rights and the right to education.

How light work found me

In April 2004, I was encouraged to see a past life regressionist by my angels to make sense of my complex life of turmoil and despair, mixed with a knowing I had something in this life to achieve. It had been a very confusing and often frustrating journey, even though I'd been seeking answers through a more spiritual-based life for ten years up to then.

So when their message came to me, I listened. *'Amanda, you're about to discover some important information which will help you understand your calling but first we want you to get in touch with someone who can create a shift in your awareness.'*

Nothing out of the ordinary seemed to jump out at me during that session, however the regressionist told me I was a 'light worker' and that in time I would understand what that entailed. I had never heard that term before and went home a little disappointed that no lightning bolt moment had occurred where I would make sense of my world.

On 16 May 2004, only a few short weeks later, at around 7 p.m., I had the most profoundly surreal experience. My children had just gone to bed as they were both under the age of three, and I was sitting watching some nonsense on television to numb my day, when everything in my environment started to shift as if I was having some hallucinogenic experience, and my angels came through with a profound message. *'Pay attention Amanda. This is now your time to understand what you're here to do and the people you're here to serve.'*

The television seemed to move backwards and the lights dimmed. Unexpectedly, a screen appeared in the room about a metre in front of me as if I was sitting in a cinema but, instead, the screen was made up of an old 35mm-camera film, complete with perforations along the top and bottom. The film reel had two spools either end and the film started to move slowly from left to right like on a conveyor belt.

For the next half an hour I was mesmerised by the unfolding experience. My angels were all around me, telling me to pay attention to the film strip. On it, I watched my unfolding future and what they wished me to see to understand my mission, what my message was to share to the world. It frightened me at first, to say the least, and I tried to rationalise as to why the experience was occurring, as I'd never had something as tangible occur like that before. I thought I'd been drugged.

Regardless of my protestations and flippant comments/ attitude, my angels were patient with me, assuring me I was ready to see this information. I, however, felt it was the last thing I needed and argued I just wanted a normal life of school runs and play dates for my children. What they showed me about my future seemed too absurd as the me on screen was someone I didn't recognise at all. However, the spools suddenly came to a grinding halt, rewound very quickly and started again with a different story. It started on the day my mother and father met. The film continued to play out in front of me as my angels showed me how my parents had been chosen to produce me as their child for me to have all the life experiences and lessons needed for me to grow into my role later in life.

Even though I pooh-poohed it, feeling I was losing the plot, I recorded what they told me later that evening and sure enough, everything my angels assured me would happen in my future actually happened.

For the next six months my spiritual growth was rapid — insane in fact. I lost four dress sizes as I was living on a light adrenalin-fuelled life and my body was responding accordingly. Even though I had been incredibly isolated, hardly leaving my home other than to attend children's activities, I found myself travelling to places all over the UK and abroad, visiting sacred sites, and I started working for a light worker, helping her with her spiritual work, and met the most knowledgeable teachers who affirmed my mission, helping me to find pieces to my unfolding jigsaw to the bigger picture.

Something happened after all in that regression and from the moment I embraced what my purpose was played out to me by my angels, my life was then dedicated to honouring my calling in bringing light into this world. My clients came from out of the blue and seemed to simply 'find me', and it started to become apparent that I was carrying out the same process with them. By helping to release them from the negative programmes of their past, it was not only allowing them to replace them with positive programmes from their blueprint, but it was activating their light. They too were becoming aware of their light worker role.

It started to become the norm as I found that every person I worked with, whatever role they had in life — whether it be an office assistant, teacher, solicitor, policeman, actor, writer, childminder, hairdresser or politician; whether they were young or old, male or female — all naturally found their purpose. This is the fundamental role of being a light worker, as I was shown by my angels that they come in all guises and become aware at different stages of their lives to work with the cosmic plan.

How to recognise everyday light work

We all come into this life ultimately to have created something of our lives and hopefully for many it's to leave a legacy in some way that perhaps will have made a difference. Some are subtle, like the volunteers that work in the soup kitchen for the homeless, carers around the world looking after elderly relatives or people in their community, nurses who go that extra mile and open their heart to their patients, a kind man on the street who helps an elderly lady across the road. In whatever way that light is served, it creates a ripple effect.

Some of those volunteers handing out hot meals could be the difference in saving lives or even inspiring those lost and homeless souls to find a better way. Those rescued souls could go on to change their lives for the better and go on to inspire others to better theirs.

Nurses have a vital role as it is, but I've experienced nurses who've known just what to say to me to make me feel protected and cared for during frightening and isolating times in hospital. I never forgot those nurses and not only are many of my friends nurses today, spreading their light, but there are those around the world, putting the heart back into nursing. And so, the ripple continues.

How do we know how that kind gentleman helping the lady over the road could have helped her that day? She could have been feeling unloved and alone in her assisted living flat and gone back with a change of heart to inspire the other residents that there are people out there who care. We've all felt alone at times in our lives, but I believe that when people reach out and share their light with others, they're passing on the light our angels have inspired in us to raise the vibration of our entire planet. As more people embrace their light, it will tip the balance to help find resolution to all the major negative situations the world faces, such as pollution, poverty, abuse, terrorism, trafficking, and so on.

Becoming a light worker

When two flames come together, they increase. When light meets light, it amplifies also. Allowing your angels of light to amplify your own light, sets that ripple in motion for a greater purpose. We all have the 'light worker essence' within us as we're all from that Divine spark that created us. Finding our 'light worker self' and purpose is key to everything we seek.

It is not an easy path by any means. Many who recognise they are light workers will testify to this. To fully embrace my role, I had to face darkness head-on in all its guises, wrestle the inner demons of my mind, take ownership of my mistakes, even when I looked stupid to others in order to redeem myself, and stand up for my beliefs when others wanted to slay me down. My angels were constantly by my side reminding me *'Amanda, embrace your truth and it will always serve you.'*

Your aim is not to be good and honourable all the time, as you are only human! It is about doing your best, taking ownership, honouring and learning from your mistakes so you can help yourself and others.

Our angels are not just there for us as messengers, protectors and guides, they also help us to understand how to bring more light into our lives for us, our loved ones and all those around us. Spreading that light creates a better world as it spreads it extensively like a ripple, moving through people we know and those we may never even meet. Angels touch our lives in order to pass the light to us like the eternal flame that many cultures and religions have used throughout history to symbolise the Divine spark from Source. When we open up to the pure radiant white light and unconditional love from our angels it is an endless gift to us, an eternal flow from Source that we can spread to whatever lives we touch. Becoming mindful of our environment and redirecting that light into our homes, businesses, communities and through the way we communicate online, can have limitless beneficial effects and create healing where it's needed.

Your light bulb moment

When I first discovered I was a 'light worker' and, not only that, that there were millions of others on the planet who had either discovered or would discover this for themselves, it was an 'aha' moment that helped me make sense of my life.

You may have already questioned your own existence, why you feel a certain way, react around certain people, feel afraid, feel joy or simply have a reaction to certain places or situations. In this activity, I'd like you to answer these few simple questions to see if you have certain characteristics which could answer whether you're a light worker too. Chances are, you were drawn to this book to find out that you are.

1. You find that people naturally open up to you and have an empathy towards others.

2. You like to have 'alone time'.

3. Sometimes you feel like an outsider.

4. You've had some kind of angelic experience.

5. You have a genuine affinity with people, animals and nature.

6. You have some kind of creative passion.

7. You feel you need to protect your sensitivities as you absorb energy like a sponge.

8. You have a desire to allow your Divine light to shine to others.

9. You smile at strangers.

So, you've probably found you answered most of these questions with a 'yes', which is not surprising, so welcome to the club. By answering 'yes' to the above questions, you may well find it a relief to know that you're not an outsider after all, but part of a hugely growing number of our collective population that's embracing their light and purpose. By reading this book now and with the help of your angels of light, it's time to honour yours.

Embrace your truth

When we seek the truth in ourselves and honour the essence of who we are, we find that peace, that abundance and the life that's destined for us, despite our preconceived thoughts about ourselves. Our truth is discovery of the self and others in a way that lets us see the multiple layers of the human condition. Those that seek outer conditioning may portray they are 'shiny happy people' but their existence relies on the perceptions of how others view them. This judgement is changeable and therefore fleeting.

Embracing change in ourselves supports the transformation our world needs to make on a grand scale. Finding our authentic true nature is our Divine calling to make this a better world to live in. By discovering our power and voice we can not only help ourselves, but we can help our loved ones and communities to live a life of authenticity and greatness which is our legacy, so we can leave a better world for those who follow.

A Note from the Author

When I first started to write this book I had no idea how much of a transformative process I would go through myself. I wholeheartedly understood why my angels of light had led me to write this but from the beginning of the writing process I realised I had agreed to step into the tunnel of possibility and change myself, in order to trust I would come out the other side as the metamorphosed person I am today.

My angels of light have always been there throughout my life, protecting and teaching me to help myself and others, loving me unconditionally. Their constant encouragement to keep honouring my yearning to write, despite the many setbacks I faced, made writing this book an especially beautiful answer to my prayers when I received the call to say I was going to write this, only days after coming out of hospital. The synchronicity was a blessing from my angels of light and I thought that my true purpose was finally beginning.

Despite the many years of yearning to write, I could never have foreseen when that would happen, when I could at last say out loud *'I'm a writer.'* In hindsight, I can clearly see that my angels of light knew exactly at what moment this book would materialise even though I had no idea that I would be conveying a message on their behalf in order to share their light.

I feel incredibly blessed that, after the many years in service I've worked on myself and others in order to grow, I am now sharing this with you. Even through the darkest moments while writing this, my angels' light was constant, shining a spotlight on whatever I needed to do in order to push through and find my power to get here. I feel extraordinarily privileged to have had this opportunity to combine all that I'm passionate about with the human condition, and my yearning to write with the love I have for my angels of light to create what I hope will bring change to your world too.

Sharing what I've learned from my dearest friends, who are my guidance system and my supporters too, has allowed me to be a voice on their behalf, sharing the innate gift that we all have to open up and allow ourselves to communicate with our angels of light to come into our lives. I feel truly gratified to be able to pass on what I've learned from them as I know that you, too, will start to see the magic and wonder of their love when you step aside from your old restrictions and let them radiate their love and wisdom to you.

What I've learned through my own personal journey while writing this book is that I am all the wiser for it, as it has been a journey of healing, transformation and unconditional love, unfolding in the most significant way. This is something I didn't expect and I feel remarkably connected to my readers because of that. My angels of light have always encouraged a deep empathy with the clients I have worked with for over twenty years. I have wondered how I could possibly feel the same connection with my readers.

Having made the decision to put all my focus and attention into writing this book, I missed the interaction of energy with my clients, missed teaching my classes, but it became apparent when the book started to unfold that my angels of light were encouraging me to write to my readers as if they were there with me in the room. The essence of that connection was palpable and at times my angels of light would assure me that I was already communicating their light to those who would eventually find this book in order to work with their own angels of light, too. You may feel that this book has spoken to you, as I have found many books have spoken to me over the years, as if they were supportive friends on my own personal journey. Many books — and films for that matter — I believe are written and created through channelled enlightenment from angels of light to share wisdom, light and healing to the world.

As the writing process began, I thought I was doing something wrong and asked my angels why the process was stirring up emotions and challenges in the way that it was, but each day I would see signs to reassure me they were guiding me and I was definitely where I should be. Sometimes I would hear a message in a song playing on the radio in answer to a concern I had; often it came in challenges when the right solutions would miraculously appear and shake up my old life which was starting to fall away. Whenever I asked them to show their presence, I would always see their glorious glowing energy as orbs and feel their presence through the tingling of my skin.

I was astounded and immensely thankful that my angels of light entrusted me to impart what they wished me to share with you and it was by no means surprising that I had to go through my own personal transformation in order to fully appreciate the essence they wished their message to relay. Being honest with you, I thought at the beginning of this journey that it would be a joyous exercise of creative expression but it turned out to be a life-changing experience that I hope has been passed on through the heart of this book, on to you too.

'Gratitude?' I said to my angels one day after I had asked how they wanted me to deal with my ridiculous feelings of insecurity stemming from all that I'd created. That word had come to me in a meditation when I was working with a group of empowered women and when I asked my angels what they meant they replied:

'Amanda, we know you are struggling with accepting what you have now. Being grateful for everything without judgement will take you beyond the uncomfortable to embrace the embodiment of who you've become.'

I was completely floored by this, thinking that I'd already overcome so many adversities, learned so much, come so far and created what I thought I wanted. In the end, this book allowed my angels to teach me that as soon as we think we know something, we don't.

There is so much expansion that we will go through, and we will continue to do so throughout our life. If we feel that we are finally there, it stops us realising that we will continue to grow as human beings when we open ourselves up to limitless possibility in response to what our angels of light are guiding us to see for ourselves.

When we reveal our truth, showing vulnerability when in a place of power, guided by our angels of light, we connect with each other at the heart level, learning valuable lessons for growth and expansion as the human race continues. We are an extraordinary race of limitless possibilities, once unlearned lessons have allowed our best selves to shine.

I hope that you will fully embrace this and give yourself every opportunity to use this book in order to give permission to your angels of light to guide you into the light.

A colour stream kaleidoscope
And urges from my soul,
I paint the canvas of my mind
To reach my highest goal.

Invitation to the Reader

I would love you to share your story with me of how this book has helped you to develop your own angel communication, how it's opened up your world to your own angels of light and how that experience has changed your life for the better.

Please send your stories to:
info@amanda-hart.co.uk

With love and light always
Amanda

About the Author

Amanda Hart has been an intuitive consultant for over twenty-two years helping people to overcome adversity, to help them find their power and voice.

By helping them to remove the negative programmes that have caused their destructive cycles in various ways, it not only helps them to align to their authentic self, but it awakens them to their innate power, healing and creative expression. Once realigned, clients find their place in this world, their people, their purpose and their peace.

Her memoir *The Guys Upstairs* quite unexpectedly changed her life having battled personally with a turbulent childhood, years of domestic violence, addictions, depression and debilitating conditions post-meningitis. Endorsed by key experts such as Professor Evan Stark (author of *Coercive Control*) and DCI Steve Jackson (National Domestic Abuse Co-Ordinator, College of Policing), she had no idea of the impact that book would have on her personally, as well as others.

Some may know her as one of the finalists on *Britain's Psychic Challenge* on Channel 5, a presenter on My Spirit Radio and columnist for *Soul & Spirit Magazine*. Today she speaks publicly about her story, to help others make sense of theirs.

Amanda works collaboratively with other inspirers from around the world and passionately supports a large global network of women, helping to elevate and empower them to stand out and fully embrace their unique purpose, to make this a better world to live in.

Her message is clear — *'Our purpose unlocks our power and voice. Embracing vulnerability leads us to fear less and love more.'*

Today her books, teaching and her campaign to raise awareness to support those suffering adversities, speaks volumes about the kind of determined commitment she has, to make this a better world to live in.

Talking with Angels of Love

How to communicate with angels of love to strengthen your relationship with yourself, others and the world around you.

Filled with practical exercises, meditations to channel your angels' love, pages to record their loving messages and touching real-life stories about the healing power of love, this book will soothe your soul and help you to trust the goodness in others again.

PUBLISHING IN JANUARY 2020

Talking with Angels of Wealth

Learn to connect with your angels of wealth and bring good fortune to your life.

With real accounts of angelic assistance, meditations, practical exercises and spaces to record the blessings sent to you by your angels, this book will help you understand the meaning of wealth and how to achieve and keep it.

PUBLISHING IN SUMMER 2020